LAW AND ECONOMY
IN PLANNING

LAW AND ECONOMY
IN PLANNING

by Walter Firey

UNIVERSITY OF TEXAS PRESS AUSTIN

Library of Congress Catalog Card No. 65–16472
Copyright © 1965 by Walter Firey
All Rights Reserved

Printed by The University of Texas Printing Division, Austin
Bound by Universal Bookbindery, Inc., San Antonio

To Paul and John

PREFACE

PLANNING has become an accepted method for bringing about improvements in community, regional, and national life. It has become a subject for study in the universities, and it has become a craft plied by skilled practitioners. But it has not become a profession.

The distinguishing mark of a profession, by which it is set off from other kinds of crafts, lies in its possession of an intellectual framework. Such a framework gives meaning to a craft, furthers a common language among its practitioners, and links practice and research to some first principles. If planning is ever to acquire the status of a profession it must first develop an intellectual framework.

The present study is an investigation of some important elements of such a framework. The elements are drawn from two disciplines, jurisprudence and economics, whose common concern with scarce means to given ends has long been apparent to social philosophers. The way in which these elements are put together to form a unified system of concepts gives the study whatever claim it may have on the attention of readers who are interested in the philosophy of planning.

Every system of concepts, of course, is subject to its own increasing entropy, mainly at the hands of perspicacious critics. I am perversely hopeful, though, that a limit to this process will have been set by the prospect that, whatever the intellectual framework of planning, it is going to be an "interdisciplinary" one. More than a dozen years of participating in an interdepartmental program of community and regional planning at The University of Texas have convinced me of the practical necessity and the intellectual possibility of such a framework. A year of concentrated study and discussion at the Center for Advanced Study in the Behavioral Sciences afforded me the incomparable opportunity to develop that opinion into a reasoned argument. It is to collegial relationships of this kind that we must look for the ecumenicity that will some day give us an adequate philosophy of planning.

WALTER FIREY

Austin, Texas

CONTENTS

LAW AND ECONOMY
IN PLANNING

CHAPTER I

The Pure Theory of Planning

All that we know of the life of man is merely a certain relation of free will to inevitability . . .

Leo Tolstoy[1]

P LANNING is an art. It is also a science. As art it is supposed to have some influence on human affairs. As science it is supposed to be predictive of human affairs. In this dual character of planning there lies a philosophical problem—the problem of free will and determinism.

If a plan really were to influence anything would we not have to conclude that there is no natural order in human events—else how could purpose shape their course? Or, if there really were a natural order in human events would we not have to deny the independent role of planning, regarding it as only an intellectual prediction of what would have happened anyway?

Quite early the Greeks saw the problem in terms of a fundamental opposition between φύσις and νόμος: nature is constant, man is arbitrary. Later, with Aristotle and then with the Stoics, man came to be seen as forming part of nature, capable of happiness just insofar as he adapts his behavior to a natural order. Subsequent formulations of the problem have nearly all been variations on these two themes.

---

[1] Leo Tolstoy, *War and Peace,* trans. by Louise and Aylmer Maude (London: Oxford University Press, 1939), Vol. III, Second Epilogue, p. 532.

Planning as a Normative Phenomenon

In neither of these classical formulations, however, has the
formal character of planning ever been at issue. Quite apart from
the problematic relation which planning bears to actual events,
there has never been any disputing the fact that it belongs to the
realm of the "ought" or the "right" rather than to the realm
of the "is." A plan, whatever else it may be, is a normative
order rather than a natural order. It is a system of propositions
which specify events that ought to be or have a right to be, as
distinct from events that are.

In addition to its fundamentally normative character there are
two further attributes of planning which have been generally
taken as essential. In the first place, a plan may or may not correspond with future events (either as cause or as prediction).
Second, there may or may not be unity among the norms which
comprise a plan. These two attributes can be given names. When
a plan on the whole does correspond with future events it may be
called an *effective* plan. When, in addition, there is some kind
of unity to the norms which comprise a plan, we may call those
norms *valid* norms; the activities which they specify are valid activities.[2] The efficacy of a plan, we shall presently find, is a necessary, though not a necessary and sufficient, condition for the
validity of its constituent norms.

Viewed in these terms the problem of free will and determinism can be given a new formulation, one that has its basis in the
pure theory of law as developed by Hans Kelsen. Specifically, the
validity of a single plan norm, taken by itself, in no way ensures
that it will bear any relationship to actual events; it may or it may
not. Validity only tells us that a particular norm is so related to
the other parts of a generally effective normative order that an

[2] These two features of a normative order are developed by Hans Kelsen in his *General Theory of Law and State,* trans. by Anders Wedberg
(Cambridge, Massachusetts: Harvard University Press, 1945), pp. 29–44.

individual who accepts the order as a whole is obliged or entitled to acknowledge the oughtness or rightness of the particular norm in question. Efficacy, on the other hand, tells us that the content of the normative order, taken as a whole, does correspond with the content of actual events. Hence, whether the content of a particular norm can be realized in empirical reality (either as cause or as prediction) depends on two things: first, whether that particular norm bears the kind of relationship with a normative order such that an individual in that order is obliged or entitled to acknowledge its oughtness or rightness; and second, whether the order to which it belongs is, taken as a whole, an effective one.

In this formulation the relationship between a plan as a normative order, and human events as a natural order, becomes one of correspondence—a relationship which is at once simpler and more agnostic than the idea of causation or prediction. The analysis which we propose to make of this correspondence between the normative and the real is going to help us resolve the dilemma of free will and determinism, so far as planning is concerned, and it will thereby enhance the prospects that planning can indeed be a rational enterprise.

The pure theory of planning, then, is a normative discipline, in the same sense that grammar and ethics are normative disciplines; its task is to provide formal categories for the analysis of a particular class of propositions, though not to prescribe or to evaluate those propositions. The theory of planning finds its subject matter in propositions that specify events which have their place in the future but which might not become real in the absence of the plan. Such propositions can be in the indicative mood or in the imperative mood, but in either case their normative character is the fundamental one. A system of incentives, for example, when given force by appropriate fiscal measures, might at first glance appear to be a set of indicative statements; yet, by virtue of their implicit recognition that an individual has the right to opt for or against them, such statements reveal their truly normative character. Administrative decrees, which take the form of imperative propositions, are even more obviously normative in character. Incentives and administrative decrees, we shall find, are the two principal instruments of planning.

The data of a pure theory of planning, then, are propositions, either actual or possible, concerning what ought to be or has a right to be. Such propositions assert a normative relationship between an individual or collectivity on the one hand and an activity on the other hand. Consider, for example, the statement: "The management of the southern branch of the Allied Units Trust ought to maintain an annual increase in production of five percent over the next six years." This statement is a normative proposition which specifies an "ought to" relationship between an individual (the management) and an activity (maintenance of a five percent annual increase in production). The intent or purpose which lies behind such a statement is that of influencing events rather than of informing us about them. Consider now the statement: "A farmer has a right to plant his land in the most profitable combination of crops." Here is a proposition that may not be quite so clearly normative. Yet consideration of the intent which lies behind the statement will reveal its essentially normative character. The statement does not tell us what farmers are doing; it tells us what they have a right to do. In such a statement the purpose, like that of the previous example, is one of influencing events rather than of informing us about them.

In both of these examples, one involving an "ought to" relationship, the other involving a "having a right to" relationship, we note an interesting parallel to the classical jurisprudential distinction between the prescribed and the permitted —a distinction which we are going to elaborate upon in the course of our later discussion. At the moment it is enough to take note of the distinction and to observe that the administrative decrees of a plan characteristically take the form of prescriptions or "ought to" propositions, whereas incentives, the other main instrument of planning, usually operate through permissions or "having a right to" propositions. Both are normative propositions.

A plan, of course, is not a utopia. Its norms do more than to merely assert what ought to be or has a right to be. They attach sanctions to these respective conditions. In this respect our two foregoing examples fail to distinguish the normative propositions of a plan from those of a utopia or an ethical system. Some further specification of plan norms must be made if these are to be accorded any special analytical status. The point of departure for such a specification has again been given us by Kelsen. Plan norms, we may say, affirm that if a specified agent (either an individual or a collectivity) does not do what is prescribed for him to do or what he is permitted to do, then another specified agent (either a collectivity or an individual) has a corresponding duty or a corresponding right, as the case may be, to employ certain specified measures with respect to the first agent. Thus a certain reciprocity is implied in the normative order of a plan whereby the violation of a prescription or the neglect of a permission by one agent implies that another agent, whom we shall call the *planner,* ought to or has a right to impose specified sanctions upon that agent.

The following example will illustrate this distinguishing feature of a plan norm: "If the management of the southern branch of the Allied Units Trust does not maintain an annual increase in production of five percent over the next six years, then the directors of that trust ought to remove the management." In this normative proposition there is a hypothetical antecedent, "If the management . . . ," and a conditional consequent, ". . . then the directors . . ." This is the typical form of an administrative order. In it an unwanted prospect x' (removal of the management) is supposed to confront the agent who is remiss in his observance of a prescribed activity x (maintenance of a production increase). Consider now the following plan norm:

"If a farmer does not plant his land in the most profitable combination of crops, then a creditor has a right to deny him a loan." Here again a hypothetical antecedent, "If a farmer . . . ," is followed by a conditional consequent, ". . . then a creditor . . ." This of course is the typical form of an incentive. In it an unwanted prospect x' (denial of a loan) is allowed to befall an agent who fails to perform a permitted activity x (planting the most profitable crops).

Plan norms are thus distinguished from other kinds of norms by their hypothetical-conditional character, a feature of legal norms first described by Kant and more fully formulated by Kelsen. The hypothetical antecedent states the possible disregard or neglect, by one agent, of a particular obligation or right; the conditional consequent specifies a sanction which some other designated agent, the planner, ought to invoke, or has a right to invoke, upon the disregard of the obligation or neglect of the right by the first agent. A plan is a set of such norms, either actual or possible, concerning a particular class of future human events. These events, it must be emphasized, fall within the realm of the "ought to be" or the "having a right to be" and have only a problematic correspondence with events in the realm of the "is." In other words the events of a plan are merely the contingent events of a normative order. They are possible rather than actual.

An *event*, in the present sense of the word, should be taken to mean a coincidence of happenings, viewed either *ex post* or *ex ante,* which have some unique space-time reference. An event (or class of events) which recurs over time may be called a *process.* In the special case where a process involves the conscious participation of its human agents it may be called an *activity.* Planning, of course, is primarily concerned with activities. Most particularly it is concerned with those activities to which an attribute of scarcity attaches, that is, with activities in which means are scarce in relation to given wants. These may be called economic activities.

Consider, for example, the prospective maintenance by a particular management of a five percent annual increase in the production of a particular commodity, together with the scales of successive annual outputs and the indicated reproportioning of productive factors which is necessary for such an increase. This entire class of events may be considered an activity, x. A plan norm, now, is a statement which specifies the complement of this activity as a hypothetical antecedent. The obligatory replacement of an unsatisfactory management by another management, at the behest of the directors of a trust, is likewise an activity, x', inasmuch as it is in principle a recurrent happening which is specified by the plan norm as a conditional consequent. Finally, the prior rate of increase in the production of a particular commodity by a particular management may properly be considered an activity—a retrospective activity which serves as reference point for the formulation of the prospective activities x or x'. Retrospective activities, like prospective activities, have of course a purely normative status within a plan, constituting part of the "ought not to be"; unlike prospective activities, however, they definitely have a counterpart in the "is," namely, in the series of recurrent events which have actually happened.

Profit-oriented farming, x, and the withholding of crop loans, x', offer additional illustrations of the term *activity* as the word is here employed. In a plan norm the complement of x, performed by a designated agent, is specified as a hypothetical antecedent, and x' is specified as a conditional consequent legitimately available to another specified agent. Any previous mode of farming, set forth in terms of proportions of productive factors and of inputs and outputs, would be a retrospective activity endowed with the normative status of "having no right to be." It too would have its counterpart in the realm of actual events.

The Epistemological Status of Planning

In this conception of a plan as a normative order we have the ingredients of a pure theory of planning. Such a theory will be an avowedly nonempirical one. Its data are not only the actual plan norms of existing and past societies but are, indeed, the logically conceivable plan norms of all possible societies. Its concern will lie with those attributes which, of logical necessity, are universally characteristic of all plans. In this respect the pure theory of planning expresses "the mathematical ideal of knowledge,"[3] an ideal whose tradition extends from Pythagoras and Plato to Descartes, Kant, and Frege in philosophy, as well as to Kelsen in jurisprudence and Walras in economics. The pure theory of planning, then, must direct its attention to form rather than content, to grammar rather than lexicography.

In this theory ". . . planned economy will have its economic laws."[4] But such laws will be no more than artifacts of the theory itself. They will be theorems that have been inferred from a set of postulates whose component concepts were imposed *a priori* upon a particular class of human events. Such laws, stating relationships that hold universally for all possible plan norms, can have only a tautological truth (though under certain conditions, stated within the theory itself, they will bear a determinate relationship with actual events). Their consistency, corresponding to the unity of each and every plan, will itself be a creation of logic and of the concepts imposed *a priori* upon events by the pure theory of planning.

The pure theory of planning finds its principal justification in the special formulation which it is able to give to the problem of free will and determinism. In it the problem has to do not with

[3] William Ebenstein, *The Pure Theory of Law* (Madison: University of Wisconsin Press, 1945), p. 15.

[4] Maurice Dobb, "Economic Theory and the Problems of a Socialist Economy," *Economic Journal*, Vol. 43 (December, 1933), p. 597.

a particular relationship between some subjective state of mind on the part of a planner and an objective course of events. Rather the problem turns on the strictly formal, logical possibility, given a properly constructed theory concerning the relationships among a number of norms, that the agents specified in those norms can, with no contradiction to any other part of the theory, be considered as bearers of an "ought" or of a "right."

In this formulation free will becomes an attribute of the normative order rather than of the natural order. Determinism, for its part, becomes an attribute of the natural order, rather than of the normative order. There is no contradiction, then, as Kelsen was first to show, in acknowledging the facts of both free will and determinism, provided one is clear about the referents of those terms.[5] Individuals *qua* individuals are never free. It is only the normative order that can be free—for it is the normative order that specifies events differently from what they might be in the natural order. This freedom of the normative order then passes over to whatever agents have been designated in the conditional consequents of the various norms which comprise an order.

What kinds of agents, now, are specified in the normative propositions of a plan? In the first clause of a normative proposition, that is, in the hypothetical antecedent, the agent is one who is supposed to be capable of either observing or violating a prescribed or permitted activity. This agent may be either an individual or a collectivity. Similarly in the second clause, the conditional consequent, the agent is one who is supposed to be capable of either exercising or waiving the duty or the right of imposing specified sanctions on the first agent. It is this agent who is the planner. He or it, like the first agent, may be either an individual or a collectivity. An agent, thus, is only a unique, singular focus of the normative order, corresponding to, but not identical with, an actual physical being or aggregate of physical

[5] Ebenstein, *The Pure Theory of Law*, p. 67.

beings. It may be a nation, a corporation, a church, a family, or an individual.

Planning, then, is not the peculiar prerogative of nations or corporations. Families and individuals plan too. Any kind of agent who is stipulated in the conditional consequent of a normative proposition as the bearer of an "ought" or of a "right" can be a planner. A plan is simply a set of normative propositions which prescribe or permit certain specified future activities. Hence there can be at least as many planners as there are plans. Any given social order will be the arena for many plans and planners, prescribing and permitting activities of the most diverse sorts, some of them compatible and some of them incompatible. Some of these plans are effective, some of them are not. In this fact lies the root of a fundamental problem which has occupied social philosophers of all times and all places. Phrased in terms of our present inquiry the problem has to do with the kind of agent which is the focus of effective plans, that is, of plans which correspond with actual future events. Do effective and noneffective plans differ significantly with respect to the kind of agent which is specified as the planner by a set of plan norms?

In a general way social philosophers can be classified into two groups according to the answer which they have given to this question. In one group are those who associate effective plans with the government or with some other collectivity that is endowed with power. In the other group are those who associate effective plans with discrete individuals. Each of the answers which these two groups have given is a variant of a particular philosophical tradition. In the first of these traditions, by no means an entirely self-conscious one, effective political action of all kinds, including planning, is made a function of collectivities. Power, sovereignty, solidarity, regulation, centralized decision-making—these are the explanatory concepts which loom large in the literature of this tradition. From Thrasymachus and Callicles through Bodin and Hobbes, the Mercantilists and the

Cameralists, Marx and von Treitschke, to Austin and Kelsen, despite the widest of differences in treatment and sophistication, there is a continuity of concern with the collectivity as the focus of an effective normative order. In the second of the two philosophical traditions, this one exhibiting more self-consciousness and continuity than the first, an effective normative order is made the function of discrete individuals freely coming to terms with one another. Liberalism, freedom, individualism, laissez faire, decentralized decision making—these are the explanatory concepts which figure most prominently in this tradition. From Glaucon and Carneades through the Epicureans, Pope Pius II, Althusius, Locke, the Physiocrats, and Adam Smith, on down to Walras, with all the variations in emphasis and elegance that one might expect, there is a continuity of concern with freely contracting individuals as the foci of an effective normative order. The same dualism in social thought can be found in the philosophical literature of other great civilizations. In China the legalist school, *fa chia,* emphasized government and authority as bases of the normative order, while the taoist school, *tao chia,* advanced a laissez-faire conception of the normative order. Mauryan India produced Kautilya's *Arthashastra,* with its remarkable analyses of sovereignty and power; the India of just two centuries earlier was the seat of Buddhism, with its democratic, social-contract theory of the normative order.

During the last two centuries of western social thought these different conceptions of the normative order have reached their culminations, respectively, in analytical jurisprudence and economic value theory. These two disciplines represent particular approaches to two more comprehensive disciplines. Analytical jurisprudence is but one approach to jurisprudence, sharing place with historical jurisprudence, realistic jurisprudence, the jurisprudence of interests, and natural-law doctrine. So too, value theory must share place in contemporary economic thought with institutional economics, macro- or aggregative economics, dynamic process analysis, and economic history. Characteristic of both analytical jurisprudence and economic-value theory is their common commitment to "the mathematical ideal of knowledge." Marking them off from one another are their differing conceptions of the normative order.

Analytical jurisprudence proceeds from the observation that a coercive aspect qualifies much of human activity. Everywhere the individual is an agent upon whom devolve specific obligations toward other individuals, and these obligations are enforced by sanctions which can be executed in the name of a collectivity. The bearer of these obligations is *Homo juridicus,* who is conceived as a purely formal artifact of the collectivity. Economic-value theory, on the other hand, proceeds from the observation that human activity bears a voluntary aspect. The individual can be viewed as an agent who possesses certain rights to want-gratification, though these rights carry with them the correlative rights of other individuals to employ countermeasures where necessary on behalf of their own want-gratification. The bearer of these rights is *Homo oeconomicus,* a purely formal creature whose contractual relations with others of his kind give rise to the collectivity.

Jurisprudence and economics are thus *in pari materia* by their common concern with economic activities—activities that partake of the attribute of scarcity. They are on equally common ground in their concern with normative orders and with the formal conditions under which such orders are effective and under which they are not effective. But they differ fundamentally with respect to the kind of agent which they postulate as the focus of an effective normative order. In analytical jurisprudence the agent which is supposed to employ the sanctions of an effective normative order is conceived to be the government or a duly constituted representative thereof. In economic-value theory the agent which has a right to employ the sanctions of an effective normative order is conceived to be the discrete individual. In the former the individual's attributes are derived by delegation from those of the collectivity; in the latter the collectivity's attributes are derived by amalgamation from those of discrete individuals. For analytical jurisprudence, micro-order proceeds from macro-order; for economic-value theory, macro-order proceeds from micro-order. Where one invokes a *summa potestas* as the instrumentality by which different individual activities acquire consistency, the other invokes an "invisible hand" as the instrumentality for effecting such consistency.

A plan, we have seen, is a particular kind of normative order, one whose component norms prescribe or permit some specified future activities. The fundamental problem which faces the pure theory of planning, then, is precisely the same problem that has divided analytical jurisprudence from economic-value theory. Are the only effective plans those of the collectivity? Or are the only effective plans those of individuals? Putting the matter somewhat differently, are individual plans effective only insofar as they derive by delegation from those of an all-powerful government? Or are governmental plans effective only insofar as they derive by amalgamation from those of freely contracting individuals? Is the pure theory of planning therefore a branch of analytical jurisprudence, or is it rather a branch of economic-value theory?

Our answers to these questions have been anticipated for us by the observation, already made, that planning can operate through either or both of two kinds of instruments: administrative decrees, and incentives. The former are typically legal in nature, the latter are typically economic. Administrative decrees, as conceptualized in analytical jurisprudence, get their validity from one particular normative order, that of the *state*. Incentives, as conceptualized in economic-value theory, get their validity from a quite different normative order, one which, for want of a better term, we may call the *market*. The state and the market, we submit, are two prototypical normative orders which, in a manner we have yet to consider, become integrated in every effective plan. Each is a set of norms having a hypothetical-conditional character. In the norms of one the agent who is specified as the planner—that is, the one who ought to impose sanctions on nonconforming agents—is the government. In the norms of the other the agent who is specified as the planner is the free individual. An effective plan is an articulation of both orders into a particular kind of suborder in which two chains, those of delegation and amalgamation, meet and form an intermediate range of effective decision making. The pure theory of planning, therefore, must be a branch of the two parent disciplines of jurisprudence and economics, and most particularly of analytical jurisprudence and economic-value theory.

We are thus driven, rather inescapably, to a consideration of those theories of jurisprudence and economics which bear most obviously upon the pure theory of planning. In the two chapters which follow we propose to examine some of these theories, specifically limiting ourselves to the particular approaches represented by analytical jurisprudence and economic-value theory. Our purpose will not be primarily that of an exegetical survey of the theories in question. Instead it will be the use of them as vehicles for expounding another theory, or at least some important aspects of such a theory. We shall find, fortunately, that such use of received doctrine does little violence to the substance of the theories in question.

The chapter which immediately follows will examine planning as a legal phenomenon. For this purpose it will consider the pure theory of law as formulated by Hans Kelsen, with due recognition of the rather special character of this approach to jurisprudence. This account will provide some formal concepts with which to analyze the plan as a legal order—as an artifact, that is to say, of the state. Then Chapter III will examine planning in terms of the theory of economic equilibrium first developed by Léon Walras, recognizing again the special character of this approach to economics. This account provides some formal concepts with which to analyze the plan as an economic order—as an artifact, that is to say, of the market.

A plan can then be regarded as a particular kind of normative suborder which occupies a definite region formed by the overlap of the state and the market as normative orders. The implications of this hypothesis will be spelled out in Chapters IV and V. Finally Chapter VI will examine the relationship between the norms of a plan and the actual behavior of its human agents, seeking to formalize the conditions under which planning can make some difference in the real world.

CHAPTER II

The Legal Component of Planning

All the good of which humanity is
capable is comprised in obedience.

John Stuart Mill[1]

PLANNING begins with an anticipation of want. It is thereby confronted with that universal problem of distribution: who is to get how much? Along with this problem it is confronted with another one: who is to enforce the distribution? These two problems, one of them economic, the other legal, point up the twofold tie which the pure theory of planning has with the disciplines of economics and jurisprudence.

In the approach to these two problems (and they are the basic ones for any theory of planning) it is convenient to start with the problem of enforcement and then turn to the problem of distribution. Since neither problem is actually prior, either by logic or genesis, it will be enough to justify the order of treatment on expository grounds alone. For this reason, then, it is well to begin the account of a pure theory of planning with an examination of the general theory of law and state as formulated by Hans Kelsen in his *Allgemeine Staatslehre* (1925) and his *Reine Rechtslehre* (1934).[2]

[1] A reference to Calvinistic thought. John Stuart Mill, *On Liberty* (Chicago: Henry Regnery Company, 1955), Gateway edition, p. 89.

[2] Together translated and revised as: Hans Kelsen, *General Theory of Law and State,* trans. by Anders Wedberg (New York: Russell and Russell, Inc., 1961). All references will be to this English edition.

The Pure Theory of Law

It is the singular contribution of Kelsen to have spelled out the presuppositions and the consequences of viewing law as a normative order which is correlative with the government as an ultimate agent of enforcement. Stated in just this way, to be sure, the idea is not a new one. A half century earlier John Austin had formulated a similar conception of law, though with considerably less sophistication and consistency. A long train of previous social philosophers had likewise recognized the close connection which holds between law and force, the most notable of them being Bodin and Hobbes. According to Bodin laws are nothing but the commands of a ruler who is possessed of full sovereign power over a people. An orderly collectivity is one which has such a ruler—one who shares his power with no one, though who very likely delegates some of it to subordinate agents. Hobbes, too, argued that laws can have only that degree of efficacy with which force endows them. In the absence of a sovereign ruler who promulgates laws and then enforces them there would be chaos. A ruler, who may be either a person or a corporate group, must have complete control over law making and law enforcement, though again he may choose to delegate some of these functions to subordinate agents. Both Bodin and Hobbes enlisted a metaphysics of natural law on their behalf, professing to see in their theories both a description of what is and a prescription of what ought to be.

With Kelsen and Austin this confusion between the normative and the factual was cleared up. Austin was first to envisage the law as a normative order whose correspondence with actual events could only be a methodological postulate and not necessarily a description of the "is." This legal order, to be sure, is one that is enforced by a sovereign authority, just as it is for Bodin and Hobbes. But Austin, unlike his forerunners, saw this sovereign authority as only an analytical construct, an assumption by means of which particular laws can be related to a conceptual unit—an agent. For Austin the distinctive mark of law lies in its being the command of such a sovereign to a group of subjects, accompanied by the threat of a sanction if the command is violated. This command may proceed directly from the sovereign or it may proceed from a subordinate but delegated authority who represents the sovereign. Linking all these entities together is the assumed attitude of "habitual obedience" on the part of a group of individuals with respect to their sovereign. The whole Austinian construct is meant to be a system of assumptions, though Austin himself lapsed all too frequently into an hypostasis of his construct, locating the sovereign, for example, in actual persons or groups of persons.

Kelsen's jurisprudence is an independent discovery of the pure theory of law, purged of all extraneous elements, and developed with a sophistication and a consistency that mark it as one of the great intellectual achievements in social science. For Kelsen, law is a normative order pure and simple. In this normative order force appears as the stipulated prerogative of the collectivity rather than of discrete individuals. Any exercise of force by an unauthorized individual is a delict which appears as a hypothetical antecedent: "if a delict be committed . . ." Joined to this clause is another one, a conditional consequent, having the general form: ". . . then a sanction ought to be imposed."[3] The delict may or may not in fact take place; the imposition of sanctions may or may not take place. The point is that they are both set down in the norms of the order as events that might take place; one of them is a forbidden use of force, the other is an obligatory use of force. Thus the order does not itself bring about conforming activities; it only says that *if* there is a negation of those activities, *then* some other specified activities, namely sanctions, ought to take place, this obligation being the unique monopoly of the collectivity. In this way Kelsen links enforce-

[3] Hans Kelsen, *What Is Justice?* (Berkeley and Los Angeles: University of California Press, 1957), p. 325. Cf. p. 238.

ment with the collectivity rather than with discrete individuals, and he makes it an activity which is specified by the propositions of a normative order rather than an activity which actually occurs in the natural order.

The state, then, becomes the pivotal concept in Kelsen's theory. For him the state is a centralized, coercive normative order. Indeed it is the law. Government is the state viewed as an agent[4]—viewed, that is to say, as the collectivity upon which devolves the obligation to impose prescribed sanctions if and when a delict is committed. State and government are thus correlative to each other, the one being a particular set of norms, the other being the same set of norms "located in" or imputed to a collective agent. To speak of the state, then, is to impose a conceptual unity upon an aggregate of legal norms; to speak of the government is to designate a conceptual carrier, an agent, for this aggregate of legal norms. All the norms of a legal order are expressions of the state—not only those which prescribe but those which prohibit too. The agent associated with this order is the government.

In this conception of the normative order there is implied a distinct theory of planning. A *Planwirtschaft* represents the special case of an economy that is administered entirely as "a budgetary unit,"[5] an economy which possesses a single, centralized decision maker in the form of a governmental planning authority. An economy of this kind operates through administrative decrees—statutes, decisions, rulings, and interpretations thereof—which specify targets, allocations, and prices for various productive factors and consumers' goods. Administrative decrees are, of course, laws, and in their totality they comprise a norma-

---

[4] This is a terminological departure from Kelsen, but it appears to do no violence to the logic of his system.

[5] Max Weber, *The Theory of Social and Economic Organization,* trans. by A. M. Henderson and Talcott Parsons (New York: Oxford University Press, 1947), p. 215.

tive order. A plan, therefore, is part of a state, and a planning authority is part of a government. A *Planwirtschaft* is a centralized, coercive normative order whose components are laws which designate a planning authority as the agent who is authorized and obliged by the government to employ specified sanctions in the case of a delict.

The norms of a *Planwirtschaft*, of course, can have validity only if the order as a whole is an effective one—if, that is to say, its content as a whole corresponds with that of actual future events.[6] But more is required for the validity of a plan norm than that it belong to an effective order. Beyond this minimum condition it must also have a particular kind of relationship with the other norms of the order if it is to be valid. The same is true of the activities which are prescribed by the norms of a plan. For the explication of this relationship Kelsen's pure theory of law reveals its full analytical power. Let us turn therefore to the question of validity, having particularly in mind the norms and activities of a governmental plan but employing for their analysis the concepts and categories which Kelsen has developed for the analysis of laws generally.

The Basic Legal Norm

A plan, we must remind ourselves, is an ideal. It is a normative order rather than a natural order. Indeed such attributes of planned activities as *value*, for instance, have their being entirely in the propositions of a normative order.[7] Likewise whatever unity a plan possesses is of a meaningful (normative) rather than a causal (natural) character. The norms of a plan have a special kind of coherence, a *Sinnzusammenhang*, which converts them from a mere collection of propositions into a recognizable unity. This unity is imposed upon it by the pure theory of law through

---

[6] Kelsen, *General Theory . . .*, pp. 41–42, 119.
[7] Kelsen, *What Is Justice?*, p. 229.

a unique Kelsenite device—the concept of the basic legal norm. To this concept is joined the idea of a filiation of norms having as their upper limit the basic legal norm and having as their lower limit the final act of execution. Between these limits is a pyramid of norms having progressively greater specificity and detail as one moves from the top to the bottom of the order. Validity is the property which accrues to a norm or an activity by virtue of its having a place in this order.

The form of a plan then may be best described as hierarchical. Administrative decrees, for example, are more specific and detailed than a statute; administrative decrees themselves may be of graded specificity as one moves downward within the plan; administrative decisions are of still greater specificity and detail; and private transactions are the most specific and detailed of all. Every norm or activity within the whole order of the plan owes its validity to norms which lie somewhere above it. This validity can be traced upward along a chain of increasingly more general and inclusive norms until one reaches a final source, the basic legal norm. Possession of validity means that the individuals whose activities are governed by the plan are obliged to acknowledge the oughtness or rightness of every norm in that plan. Whether the content of their activities does in fact correspond to that of each and every norm is another matter. So long as the plan as a whole corresponds to actual events the fact of a non-correspondence between a single norm of that plan with actual events does not nullify the validity of the norm in question.

A plan, furthermore, is a dynamic order, just like the larger legal order of which it is a part. New norms are forever acquiring validity and old ones are losing it. The processes by which validity is acquired or lost have a pattern all their own. It is a merit of Kelsen's jurisprudence that it provides a formal schema for analyzing the dynamics by which plan norms are created and annulled, by which, that is to say, they acquire validity and lose validity. These dynamics consist not of an inference or deduction from premises to conclusions. Rather they consist of a procedure, stipulated by some higher norm, whereby lesser norms are supposed to come into being. A plan, in other words, is a self-regulating order; it sets forth within itself the procedures by which it is going to evolve, including therein the agents who will be authorized to create new norms. Every norm within a plan owes its validity to the fact of having been created by agents and according to procedures that have been authorized by some higher norm within the plan itself. The higher norm is thus the source of the lower norm's validity. Acquisition of validity is a one-way process, starting with the general and moving to the specific. At the beginning there is the basic legal norm, at the end there is the final act of application. Between these upper and lower limits every norm within a plan can be viewed, on the one hand, as an application of a more general norm and, on the other hand, as a source of some more specific norms. Between these limits too there is a chain of authorities—agents who have been invested by some higher norm, either directly or by delegation, with the obligation to promulgate lower norms which thereupon have full claim to validity. Validity is thus a procedural matter; it is an attribute which a norm takes on through having been created by an authorized agent according to an authorized procedure. This is what gives a norm its place in the order of a plan. Annulment of a norm comes about in exactly the same way; validity ceases only when an authorized agent, acting according to procedures spelled out by a higher norm, cancels or replaces a lower norm.

For the origins of validity, then, we must look to the upper limit of a normative order, to the basic legal norm. Since a plan is a proper subset of a legal order we cannot expect to find the basic legal norm within the plan itself. Rather we must look to the apex of the whole legal order. In doing so we shall find ourselves making explicit an intellectual device which, following Kelsen, we have all along been using though without as yet acknowledging it. According to Kelsen the basic legal norm, which is the ultimate source of validity of a law, and which gives to the legal order its very unity, is not a datum of observation at all. It is a postulate. It is an assumption which we have to make if we are to see the legal order as a unity. The function of the concept is to permit our seeing in an aggregate of norms the one particular order whose stipulated activities more nearly correspond to actual events than do the stipulated activities of any alternative order which we could see on the basis of a different postulate. The validity of this basic legal norm derives from the investigator; the validity of all other norms within a legal order derives from the basic legal norm. The basic legal norm is simply the proposition "... that one should act in obedience to the commands of the supreme authority and of the authorities delegated by it, and that these commands must be interpreted as a meaningful whole."[8] It may be more formally stated as follows: *If the command of a supreme authority be violated, then coercive sanctions ought to be applied by that authority.*[9]

The full import of this concept can be seen on a little reflection. The concept ties the validity of a normative order to one fundamental condition of its efficacy. Specifically it states that an order will be valid only if the coercion which it specifies is made the monopoly of a "supreme authority." The basic legal norm vests the exercise of force—which in the natural order is going to be exercised by someone anyway—in the government or in a duly authorized representative thereof. In Kelsen's own words, "... the basic norm ... means the transformation of power into law."[10] The ubiquitous use of force in the realm of the "is" thus finds explicit recognition in the realm of the "ought to be," by being specified in the basic legal norm as the ultimate prerogative of a

[8] Kelsen, *General Theory* . . ., pp. 405–406.

[9] The briefer version that "one should act in obedience to the commands of the supreme authority . . ." is simply the contrapositive of this formal version.

[10] Kelsen, *General Theory* . . ., p. 437.

particular kind of agent, namely, the government. All those norms which owe their validity to a basic legal norm thereby constitute a legitimized coercive order. A plan is just such an order.

From the fact that validity proceeds in a single direction downward from a higher norm to a lower norm we must not infer that some unique determinism is at work selecting out one and only one lower norm whose content can be compatible with a given higher norm. Quite the contrary. Every norm admits of a variety of applications. This may be either through design or through oversight. In either case there has to be an interpretation, by some authorized representative of the government, of every norm in an order, the result being a multitude of lower norms each of which, while owing its validity to some higher norm, is not at all determined by that norm. Consequently every plan has a co-efficient of indeterminacy, when we view it from the standpoint of the legal order. The creation of new norms must indeed take place according to procedures that have been specified by higher norms, but these procedures invariably allow some margin of latitude for the exercise of interpretation. Knowing the historical content of the basic legal norm from which a plan derives its validity in no way enables a prediction of the content of all the norms in that plan.

Legal Transactions and the Limits to Authority

This fact has far-reaching implications for a pure theory of planning. Their full reach will become apparent after the analysis of the plan as an economic order, in Chapter III. A prospectus of these implications, however, is afforded us by Kelsen's concept of the legal transaction. This is a norm (or set of norms) voluntarily formed in the manner of a compact by a number of free agents (whose authority to do so has been set forth by higher norms in the plan or in the legal order), and specifying in hypothetical-conditional fashion certain future activities that ought to take place. The contract is the prototypical form of a legal transaction. The validity of a contract, like that of any other legal norm, traces back through the higher norms of a plan on up to the basic legal norm. What distinguishes it from other norms, however, is the fact that the agents who have been authorized to create it are discrete individuals. In a literal sense, to be sure, these individuals are serving in the capacity of governmental representatives. Moreover, the sanctions which any one of them can invoke against the other in the case of the latter's dereliction are vested squarely in the government. The legal transaction, therefore, is an integral part of a plan. Yet it is a norm that has been freely arrived at by two or more discrete individuals. A contract between two persons, for example, becomes a norm once it has been signed by the parties concerned. Insofar as these individuals have been authorized by a higher norm to enter into such an agreement, the norm which they have thereby created is a valid one. It has a place in the plan. As such it is part of the state. At the same time, though, that contract is part of another kind of order, one which we have not as yet described, namely, the market. It is part of an order whose agents are discrete individuals. This order, as we shall presently see, has its own distinctive properties which have been most elegantly formulated in Walras' general equilibrium theory. In the legal transaction we have a legal form which partakes of a nonlegal normative order. In the legal transaction, therefore, we have a nexus between the state and the market.

From the fact that validity proceeds in a single direction downward from a higher norm to a lower norm we may draw one extremely important inference. The agents who are authorized to create norms obviously cannot be equal in respect to their authority; some of them stand in closer proximity to the supreme authority than do others. Hence, insofar as the norms which they create are effective, they cannot be equal in respect to power, for power is the counterpart in the realm of the "is" of what authority is in the realm of the "ought to be." The supreme authority which is specified in the basic legal norm as the agent empowered to impose sanctions is indeed the supreme authority. It is the government. And it is the government which has authority to enforce conformity to the content of the basic legal norm and, perforce, to that of every one of the lower norms of the order, since they all owe their validity to the basic norm. Other agents are authorized to enforce conformity to lower norms only, and then strictly by delegation from the government. Insofar, then, as the norms of a plan are effective (and most of them must be if the order as a whole is to be effective), the power of various individuals and collectivities will vary with the generality or the specificity of the respective norms which specify them as sanctioning agents. The government as a collectivity will have more power than any other agent, the planning authority will have somewhat less power, a zoning authority will have still less power, and so on down the hierarchy, with the discrete individual, considered in his strictly legal capacity, having least power of all.

Not even the government, however, and certainly no other agent, has unlimited power. For—again assuming an overall correspondence between the "is" and the "ought to be," without which the plan would not be effective anyway and its norms could not be valid—every agent derives his authority ($\equiv$ power) from one and the same basic legal norm. All his rights and duties, so far as he is an agent of a plan, are conferred upon him by the plan itself or by the larger legal order of which it is a part. Consequently every agent—even the government—finds its authority bounded by specified limits.[11] For the government these limits are set by the historically given content of the basic legal norm. For other agents the limits are set with ever decreasing scope by lower norms of the order.

This self-limiting character of a legal order, together with the

[11] *Ibid.*, pp. 93–99.

significance of the legal transaction as a special type of norm which is created by discrete individuals, provides another crucial link with that other normative order to which we shall presently turn our attention, namely, the market. For if the state is everywhere a self-limiting normative order, then there must everywhere exist some residual class of norms which will correspond to those empirical activities which are not fully governed by the state. Indeed, we shall find that the scope of the market's control over economic activities is inversely related to the scope of the state's control. Where the state is severely self-limiting, thereby assigning more authority to individuals as autonomous agents who are empowered to bargain and contract freely with one another in *ad hoc* deals, the market takes on correspondingly greater significance as an effective normative order.

Insofar as planning is part of the state, however, it becomes in that measure identified with the government as an agent of enforcement. The state is the normative order which pre-empts the use of force in the realm of the "is" and recognizes it in the realm of the "ought to be" as something that is reserved for the collectivity rather than for discrete individuals. The link between the "is" and the "ought to be" is provided by the basic legal norm. This, we have seen, is a postulate rather than a datum of observation. Yet we are not free to devise any basic legal norm that we please. There can be only one such norm which will allow us to perceive the particular unity in a set of norms which will be at once effective and valid. The import of this norm, of course, is that an effective plan will be one whose stipulated activities correspond to those which can for the most part be enforced anyway. The basic legal norm, in effect, is the device by which we acknowledge that, within limits, might makes right. Any alternative construction which we might choose to make would yield a plan that would lack the minimum requirement of validity, namely efficacy.

Thus in positing the basic legal norm we are ultimately

driven to a consideration of some existential features of planning. Our precept must be the Kantian principle that the "ought to be" of a normative order can make sense only if it corresponds to the "can" of the natural order. No order could be valid, in other words, if its norms enjoined the impossible. At the same time an order would be redundant if it enjoined the inevitable.[12] Somewhere between these two extremes there is a range of the possible-but-not-inevitable, and within this range—the range of the "can" —there is a smaller range of the "ought to be." The empirical regularities which operate within the range of the "can" have to be known if any particular normative order that we construct, falling within the range of the "ought to be," is to be an effective and hence a valid one. The question which now emerges is this: does Kelsen's basic legal norm, by itself, suffice for the task of coordinating the empirical regularities of the natural order with the formal regularities of a plan as a normative order? Or do we need another basic norm, specifically a basic economic norm, to complement his device? This is the next problem for consideration.

[12] *Ibid.*, pp. 120–121. William Ebenstein, *The Pure Theory of Law* (Madison: University of Wisconsin Press, 1945), p. 67.

CHAPTER III

The Economic Component of Planning

Thus we are born free as we are born rational.

John Locke[1]

AT THIS POINT a system of categories for a pure theory of planning begins to emerge. But the concepts so far discussed bear on only one of the two classes of events with which such a theory must be concerned: the class of legal events. An additional and quite distinct class of events, the economic, concerns who is to get how much. Relative to this problem the concepts of Kelsen's pure theory of law are not sufficient. We must look to another discipline, that of economics, for concepts which will be adequate to representing quantities of commodities and the processes of their distribution.

More than any other social science economics has reached a degree of closure in its theoretical schema. The capstone to its conceptual edifice was provided by Léon Walras in his *Éléments d'économie politique pure* (1874),[2] though it has remained for others to set this capstone firmly in place. It was the achievement

---

[1] John Locke, *Of Civil Government* (New York: E. P. Dutton & Co., 1924), Everyman's Library, Book II, Chapter VI, Section 61.

[2] Translated as: Léon Walras, *Elements of Pure Economics*, trans. by William Jaffé (London: George Allen and Unwin, Ltd., 1954). All references are to the English edition.

of Walras to have constructed a set of equations defining an abstract state of equilibrium among all the quantities of goods
and productive factors that comprise an economic system. By this
achievement Walras and his successors have shown that it is formally possible for a normative order whose foci are discrete individuals to meet an important condition of efficacy, namely, the
observable capacity of people to compare alternatives. The market
is just such an order.

The Theory of General Economic Equilibrium

Walras' performance stands as the culmination of a rich philosophical tradition whose principal strands, utilitarianism and natural harmony, had already been coordinated, though rather imperfectly, by John Locke. Locke supposed individuals to be endowed with certain inherent rights which exist independently
of the normative order and prior to it. These rights, however,
can be most conveniently secured by means of a legal order whose
every characteristic derives from the consent of a majority of its
individual agents. The resulting order articulates a basic harmony
of interests which prevails among all people; in protecting the
rights of one person the legal order is perforce promoting the
good of all.

This blending of utilitarian and harmonist thought was carried
further by Adam Smith. He, too, supposed that all individuals
possess some inherent attributes prior to their participation in the
normative order. Among these are the motives of self-love and
sympathy. According to Smith there exists between these motives
a natural balance which ensures that every individual, in pressing
for his own private advantage, will automatically serve the advantage of others as well. This harmony of interests is facilitated
by the division of labor and the resulting exchange of goods and
services among people. By specializing in certain commodities
and not in others an individual can increase his own productive
efficiency. At the same time, though, he becomes dependent on

others for the commodities in which they have specialized. The result is an exchange of goods and services in which each individual, by furthering his own advantage, perforce furthers that of others as well. In this exchange there is a tendency for goods and services to be priced in proportion to the amount of labor that is invested in them, though actual market price, determined by supply and demand, can oscillate around this natural price. The entire construct is one in which an "invisible hand" guides individuals through self-interest to serve the common good.

The special idea of an equilibrium among economic quantities—the idea that macro-order can emerge out of micro-order through a system of market prices—had been glimpsed by a number of writers before Walras, particularly by Turgot, Isnard, von Thünen, Say, Beccaria, and Cournot. Subsequent to Walras there have been several economists, notably Robinson, Keynes, and Novozhilov, who have modified the idea of equilibrium away from the extremely individualistic assumptions of the Walrasian construct. Nevertheless, as a limiting-case formulation of the market as a prototypical normative order, the work of Walras, perfected by Pareto, Hicks, Samuelson and others, stands as an apogee of theoretical development.

Walras' pure economics, like Kelsen's pure theory of law, is a formal discipline. Its laws are artifacts of the investigator's logic.[3] As such they are of tautological, and therefore universal, validity. Again like Kelsen's jurisprudence, Walras' economics is analytical rather than empirical; its data include not only observable economic norms but also the whole universe of logically conceivable economic norms. Finally, like Kelsen, Walras adds some dynamic features to his fundamentally static account of the normative order; Walras' economics provides a formal schema for

[3] *Ibid.*, p. 71. Cf. Lionel Robbins, *An Essay on the Nature and Significance of Economic Science* (London: Oxford University Press, 1932), pp. 109–110.

analyzing the dynamics by which economic norms acquire and lose validity.

Walras' pure economics describes a normative order whose propositions specify discrete individuals as the bearers of particular rights to want-gratification.[4] Individuals, therefore, with their *ex ante* attributes (wants, and various initial quantities of means), are taken as given, and formal conditions are set forth under which specified attributes of the collectivity (equilibrium quantities and proportions of means) are acquired *ex post* by a process of amalgamation from the attributes of individuals. Individuals are depicted as self-contained, autonomous units of decision having no conflicts of interest with one another and facing no inequalities of power among one another. They are assumed to be numerous enough so that no one of them can, by himself, exert a perceptible influence upon the others. The wants of these individuals are assumed to exceed the means that are available to them for their gratification. Hence each individual, in order to maximize his want-gratification up to the limit of the means available to him, must arrange his wants on a scale of preferability. Then, by entering into exchange relations with others, the individual can rearrange his own complement of means so as to maximize the gratification of his wants in the order of their worth to him. An equality between the aggregate of wants for which a group of individuals are able to procure means and the aggregate of means that are actually available to them (that is, an equality between aggregate demand and aggregate

[4] Walras, of course, regarded his system as a scientific rendition of empirical reality. In his words, "All these theories are, admittedly, abstract; but when they are progressively enfolded in one another by a process of systematic synthesis, they take us right into the midst of reality" (Walras, *Elements of Pure Economics*, p. 207). Yet Walras does acknowledge that equilibrium ". . . is an ideal and not a real state" (p. 224). Throughout our exposition we have freely substituted the idiom of normative analysis for Walras' own "positive" treatment.

supply), will result in a hypothetical distribution of means, including productive factors as well as consumers' goods, which will most fully satisfy the wants of all individuals concerned. This hypothetical distribution of economic quantities is called a general market equilibrium. At general market equilibrium the plans of various individuals have become sufficiently compatible with one another so that no one individual has both the desire *and* the ability to alter the indicated distribution of consumers' goods and productive factors.

The market is a normative order in which every economic activity which comports with a general equilibrium is classed as having a right to take place; all other activities are classed as not having a right to take place—quite apart, of course, from any actual state of affairs which might exist in natural reality. The norms which comprise the market are asking-prices and, derivatively, the individual market schedules and the collective supply and demand schedules which relate various quantities of one commodity (or class of commodities) *offered* as exchange, to various quantities of another commodity (or class of commodities) *forthcoming* in exchange.[5] For our purposes an asking-price— more briefly, a price—may be defined as a normative proposition which consists of two clauses: (1) an implicit hypothetical antecedent: If any one of a designated class of individuals does not offer a specified quantity of commodities as a bid for some specified quantity of another commodity presently held by another given individual, . . . and (2) an implicit conditional consequent: . . . then the second individual has a right to withhold a specified quantity of his commodity as means that might otherwise have been made available to the first individual. Thus a price (or an individual market schedule or a collective supply-and-demand schedule) is a permissive norm which specifies a

[5] Walras' "traders' schedules" (Walras, *Elements of Pure Economics,* p. 93).

discrete, freely contracting individual as the agent who has the right to reject terms of exchange which he deems unfair. The quantities specified in such a price are unique to the individual who bears the norm; they constitute *his* norm—the norm which he will carry with him into the market on any given occasion. An aggregate of such prices, borne by a plurality of agents, constitutes a market.

The market, we may conclude, is an aggregate of asking-prices, each of which authorizes its agent to withhold specified quantities of a commodity if certain specified terms of exchange are not forthcoming. Like Kelsen's state, the market is an intellectual construction by means of which an observer seeks to impose conceptual unity upon an aggregate of possible norms. But unlike the state, with its centralized, coercive character, the market is a decentralized, voluntary normative order. Its norms are asking-prices; in the vernacular of present-day economics they are particular, unique entries in individual market schedules, as well as the individual schedules themselves and the collective supply-and-demand schedules which derive by amalgamation from them. The validity of these norms traces upward from a postulated basic economic norm, through individual market schedules and collective supply-and-demand schedules, on up to a universal general norm of exchange, which we shall presently describe.

The theory of planning implied in this conception of the normative order is a rather different one from that implied in Kelsen's jurisprudence. A market represents the special case of an economy which operates through a plurality of independent decision makers. Such an economy involves a decentralized type of planning in which a great many individuals, competing among themselves for a limited supply of means, present one another with various prices which in the long run converge toward a state of general market equilibrium. Such prices, we have said, are norms, and in their totality they comprise a decentralized, voluntary, normative order, the market.

The Basic Economic Norm

Asking-prices, like the norms of any order, are valid only if the order to which they belong is effective. In other words, the activities which they designate as having a right to take place must, on the whole, correspond in content to the actual events of the natural order. But more is required for their validity than this. In addition to belonging to an effective order they must possess some meaningful consistency which endows them with a formal unity. In the case of prices the criterion of consistency is provided by what, to paraphrase Kelsen, we may call the basic economic norm.[6] It is the basic economic norm which determines whether or not a particular price is a valid norm, in the sense of having a place in an interconnected system of prices. The basic economic norm, like the basic legal norm, is a postulate rather than a datum of observation. It is a proposition which sets forth the criterion by which any price within a universe of prices can be considered as valid or not valid.

The basic economic norm may be stated as follows: *If means are offered to an individual which are not those he is asking for, then that individual has a right to either accept or reject the offer with a view to organizing his own complement of means into activities which will maximize his utility.* More briefly: an individual has a right to be rational. By means of this postulate we are able to perceive a special kind of unity among all the prices which comprise a market—a unity in which every price which conforms to the basic economic norm is a valid price—provided, of course, that the market is an effective order. The unity of decentralized planning—in other words, the unity of the market— is thus an artifact of our assuming as valid the basic economic

---

[6] Cf. the suggestion of a basic economic norm, somewhat different from ours, in William Ebenstein, *The Pure Theory of Law* (Madison: University of Wisconsin Press, 1945), p. 93.

norm of rationality. This unity may, with Walras, be characterized as the state of general market equilibrium.

The validity of prices, as economic norms, traces upward from that of the basic economic norm—quite in contrast to the validity of laws, which traces downward from that of the basic legal norm. So too, where delegation is the procedure by which validity accrues to legal norms, amalgamation is the analogous procedure for economic norms. It is in the formal analysis of amalgamation that Walras' performance stands out as truly epochal. His achievement was to construct a system of equations, linking together prices and quantities of commodities, which is formally consistent with a general market equilibrium. In this system of equations a particular set of prices, out of a universe of possible prices, gets selected out as valid. They are the only prices which are consistent with the basic economic norm of rationality and which, by virtue of that fact, have a place in the market as a normative order. Likewise the quantities of consumers' goods and productive factors which are associated with those prices are the only quantities that are compatible with equilibrium.

The Walrasian conditions of equilibrium can be stated, after Hicks, as follows:

I. For every individual, viewed as consumer, utility (want-gratification) must be maximized up to the limit of his means, prices being taken as given. Utility is maximized when one's stock of consumers' goods is so organized that the price ratio of any pair of them is equal to the marginal rate of substitution between them (this latter term being the amount of one commodity which can be substituted for a unit of the other without altering the individual's total utility).[7]

[7] J. R. Hicks, *Value and Capital*, second ed. (London: Oxford University Press, 1946), p. 20; Paul Anthony Samuelson, *Foundations of Economic Analysis* (Cambridge, Massachusetts: Harvard University Press, 1947), pp. 97–100; cf. Walras, *Elements of Pure Economics*, Lesson 11.

II. For every individual, viewed as producer, profit must be maximized (disutility must be minimized), subject to the limitations of a production function which describes the technical conditions of production (by relating amounts of productive factors to amount of product), prices again being taken as given. Profit is maximized when an individual's stock of productive factors and products is so organized that the price ratio between any pair of factors is equal to the marginal rate of substitution between them; when the price ratio between any pair of products is equal to the marginal rate of substitution between them; and when the price ratio between any factor and any product is equal to the marginal rate of transformation between the factor and the product (these quantities being the amounts of one factor [or product] which can be substituted for [or transformed into] one unit of another factor [or product] without destroying equality between price, on the one hand, and the added cost of increasing the output of a product by one unit, on the other hand).[8]

III. Prices must equate aggregate supply (sales) and aggregate demand (purchases) for every commodity (whether a productive factor or a consumers' good) in the market. This condition ensures that the maximum utilities and profits of all individuals will be mutually compatible.

Assuming, now, that demand is a decreasing function of price and that supply is an increasing function of price, and assuming too that the equations which link prices and quantities of commodities are linear, there can then be a unique set of prices (and a corresponding unique set of quantities of commodities) which will form a stable equilibrium. In such an equilibrium every price will tend, if varied, to return to its unique, stable value.[9] It be-

[8] Hicks, *Value and Capital*, p. 86; Samuelson, *Economic Analysis*, pp. 81–89; cf. Walras, *Elements of Pure Economics*, Lesson 18.

[9] Walras' equations do not ensure the existence of an equilibrium, in the sense of always having an economically realistic solution, nor do they ensure that an equilibrium, if it exists, will be either unique or

comes, in short, a valid norm. A set of such prices comprises a unified normative order—the market.

Yet the unity of this order, we must remind ourselves, is an artifact of the proposition which we took to be the basic economic norm—the norm of rationality. This proposition is only a convention of economic theory. The justification for selecting it, rather than some other proposition, as the basic economic norm hinges entirely on whether the normative order which follows from it corresponds more nearly in content with actual events than the order which would follow from any alternative proposition that we might have selected as the basic economic norm. In other words the order which follows from the basic economic norm must on the whole be an effective one. For efficacy, we have seen, is the minimum requirement that an order must meet if its norms are to be valid. Walras' theory of general market equilibrium ties the validity of an economic order to an assumed condition of efficacy; it implies that an economic order will be valid if its norms are consistent with the empirical fact that people do compare alternatives. The normative counterpart to this feature of the natural order is the right of every individual to be rational.

Granting the validity of the basic economic norm, Walras has given us a pure theory of planning—more generally, a pure theory of the market—in which a collective ordering of activities emerges, by amalgamation, from a multitude of individual orderings of activities. Once we know, for instance, just how each individual in a population of individuals has rated his various wants in relation to one another, we can proceed to construct his individual market schedule and, from an aggregate of such individual schedules, we can then construct aggregate supply-and-

---

stable. Such specification requires the addition of further conditions which have only recently been given satisfactory formulation. See Takashi Negishi, "The Stability of a Competitive Economy: A Survey Article," *Econometrica,* Vol. 30 (1962), pp. 635–669.

demand schedules, from which in turn we are able to arrive at a price which, for the situation at hand, will be a valid norm: it is an equilibrium price. A set of such prices for various commodities will correspond to the *collective* rating of the wants which were initially registered in the various *individual* ratings. Both ratings, of course, have a normative status: the collective rating is valid because the various individual ratings are valid. Likewise the quantities of commodities which correspond to the prices in question have a normative status: the equilibrium quantities and proportions of means are valid because the various individual arrangements of means are valid. In short, Walras' pure economics gives us a theory of the normative order that specifies just which economic activities have a right to be and which activities do not have a right to be, provided we assume the basic economic norm of rationality along with the various other special conditions that are set forth by the theory.

In very generalized form, then, a valid price may be thought of as a hypothetical-conditional proposition: if one individual offers another individual a non-equilibrium quantity of commodities as a bid for some specified quantity of a commodity presently held by the latter, then this second individual has a right to restrict the range of alternative means which would otherwise have been available to the first individual, by oversupplying or undersupplying the first individual's demand for the specified commodity. More briefly: an individual has a right either to reject or to exploit a nonequilibrium offer. This proposition may be taken as a universally valid general norm of production and exchange. The consequent clause of the proposition specifies a sanction which a designated agent has a right to employ *if* another activity (a nonequilibrium offer), specified in the antecedent clause, should actually take place. The right to employ the specified sanction attaches to a discrete individual as an autonomous, freely contracting agent. He is the planner. The sanction which the proposition authorizes him to use has the supposed effect of penalizing another individual, the first individual, for his possible nonrationality—for his possible failure to make an equilibrium offer to the second individual.

The Contract and the Limits to Rationality

Prices, like other norms, are created by the agents of a normative order. They are created by agents who are observing a right which has been given them by the basic economic norm—the right to be rational. One of the corollaries of this right is the right of every individual to form contracts with other individuals, each such contract having the general form of a norm or set of norms. Yet this right entails consequences which are quite beyond the purview of Walras' pure economics, even though they remain entirely within the normative rather than the natural order of things. A contract, if it is to be anything more than a redundant announcement by its signatories of their respective terms of exchange, must have an obligatory character. A contract, in other words, does more than specify events which have a right to take place; it specifies events which ought to take place. As such, a contract belongs not only to the market; it belongs also to the state.

To account for this dual affiliation of the contract, as a type of norm, we must look briefly at the dynamic aspect of Walras' theory. Equilibrium, we will recall, is predicated upon an equality between supply and demand for every commodity. If a particular price does not equate supply and demand it will tend, in an effective order, to be succeeded by one that does. Walras schematized the process after the model of an auction, wherein various prices are called out in rapid succession until an equilibrium price is eventually reached. To sustain this choice of the auction as a model Walras had to suppose that exchanges would not take place at any of the nonequilibrium prices; to suppose otherwise would have involved the consequence that individuals' marginal rates of substitution would be altered by their exchanging or producing at a nonequilibrium price, so that those individuals would make an approach to subsequent negotiations different from that they would otherwise have made, causing the whole conception of a final equilibrium price to be contingent upon the fortuitous facts of history and as such an entirely indeterminate quantity. To escape this consequence Walras supposed that exchange at nonequilibrium prices had only a tentative and therefore noncommittal character.[10]

It is not necessary for us to leave the realm of the "ought to be" and the "having a right to be," or to lapse into an empirical refutation of this construction, in order to see its limitations. By itself the construction is not inconsistent with the basic economic norm. But it is *prima facie* inconsistent with any other possible normative order that we might construct. Not only does it exclude our conceiving as valid any exchange which is at a price that is nonequilibrium *in retrospect*—and this quite properly; but it excludes our conceiving as valid any exchange (such as that set forth in a contract) which is at a price that *might* be nonequilibrium *in prospect*. It denies normative status to an activity that is equilibrative at the time that a transaction is closed but which becomes disequilibrative before the activity is consummated. In short, the construction excludes our according normative status to an activity which appears mutually advantageous to certain parties at the time that a contract is signed but which in the course of time becomes disadvantageous to one of those parties. True—both of the parties still have a right to observe their pledged terms, but for one of them that "right" has become contrary to his basic right to be rational. Is the activity thereupon devoid of any normative status whatsoever?

The question thus posed brings us back full circle to the hypothesis which was stated briefly in the previous chapter, namely, that the contract is a nexus between two distinct normative orders

[10] Walras, *Elements of Pure Economics*, pp. 169–172, 242.

—the economic and the legal, the "having a right to be" and the "ought to be." The contract is a norm whose validity derives from two basic norms: the basic economic norm, which states the individual's right to be rational, and the basic legal norm, which states his obligation to obey a supreme authority.

In this light it is quite possible for an activity which has been prescribed by a contract to cease "having any right to be" and to still retain its normative status: the status of the "ought." *Pacta sunt servanda.* By the same token it is possible for an activity which, at its very inception, "had no right to be"—given of course the basic economic norm of rationality—to nevertheless have some normative status—again, the status of the "ought." This is a frequent feature of governmental plans. A governmental plan, in a sense, is a contract in reverse. Where a voluntary contract between individuals begins with a dual normative tie (the "right" and the "ought") and may end with only one (the "ought"), a governmental plan begins with a single normative tie (the "ought") and may end with two (the "ought" and the "right"). Particularly in an economic development plan, where draconian measures may have to be invoked in order to bring about a desired rate of capital formation, individuals may readily acquiesce to obligatory "terms of exchange," motivated by the prospect that newly transformed factors of production will afford them a future general market equilibrium that is on a far higher level than the general market equilibrium which might be attained in the absence of the plan. Thus what was initially disadvantageous (in terms of want-gratification) for some of the agents of the governmental plan ends up being advantageous for all of them. In this way the activities which correspond to a plan acquire a dual normative status: that of "having a right to be" as well as that of the "ought to be."

A full explication of this hypothesis must be deferred to another chapter. But there is one implication of it which deserves comment now. The phenomenon of the contract, it appears, represents a limit to the analytical power of Walras' economics. Just as Kelsen's pure theory of law specifies a limit to the scope of the state as an effective normative order, so Walras' pure theory of economics must allow some limit to the scope of the market as an effective normative order. This limit is set by the Walrasian requirement, already noted, that there can be no inequality in power among the individuals who are specified as the agents of a contract; otherwise one of the agents does not have the chance to be fully rational. By itself, to be sure, this requirement is quite consistent with Kelsen's characterization of the legal transaction, of which the contract is the prototypical form. But it is not consistent with the Kelsenite concept of a supreme authority and the associated concept of a filiation of delegated authorities having lesser degrees of authority.

Here, then, is the limit of the market. The efficacy (and therefore the validity) of its norms is bounded by an empirical fact, in the natural order, of which the basic economic norm cannot take account: the fact that in certain kinds of economic activities there are power differences among individuals and collectivities. By the same token the efficacy (and therefore the validity) of legal norms, comprising in their aggregate the state, is bounded by the empirical fact that certain kinds of economic activities are not characterized by power differences among individuals and collectivities. Both limits derive from the fact that no norm can be valid unless the order to which it belongs is, by and large, an effective one. The efficacy of an order, for its part, is an artifact of the basic norm which we have assumed and from which all the other norms of the order have been derived.

At this point the problem considered in the introduction of the survey of the legal and the economic components of planning reappears: the problem of the formal conditions under which various kinds of normative orders are effective and ineffective. In particular, what are the conditions for the efficacy of a plan as a normative order? What kind of agent must be postulated as the

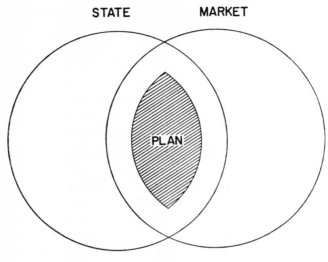

FIGURE I

focus of an effective plan: discrete individuals having the right to
be rational, or a collectivity having the obligation to enforce
obedience? The basic economic norm, which states the first alternative, is capable of yielding an effective normative order only on
the condition that it comports with complete equality in power
among its individual agents. The basic legal norm, which states
the second alternative, is capable of yielding an effective normative order only on the condition that at least some of its stipulated
activities entail unequal degrees of authority among its authorized
agents. How can planning accommodate to such different kinds of
normative orders?

Our hypothesis, which is to be developed at length in the remaining chapters of this study, may be put in the following
words: (1) the state and the market represent partially over-
lapping normative orders; (2) a plan is a normative suborder
which is situated within the overlap of the state and the market

(see Figure 1). Alternatively the hypothesis can be stated thus: a plan is a normative order whose component propositions specify some future activities which partake both of the "ought to be" and the "having a right to be." Its essence, more precisely, lies in laws-and-prices. A plan does not include propositions which specify the impossible, whether the "ought to be" or the "having a right to be," for that would be a utopia rather than a plan. Neither does a plan include propositions which specify the inevitable, whether the "ought to be" or the "having a right to be," for that would be a prophecy rather than a plan. Nor, finally, is a plan constituted by propositions which specify only the "ought to be" or only the "having a right to be," for it is the conjunction of these imperatives which distinguishes plan norms from other kinds of laws, on the one hand, and from other kinds of prices, on the other hand. An effective plan will turn out to be a normative order which assures rationality to its individual members, though only within limits, and at the same time exacts obedience of those individuals to a supreme authority, this again within limits.

The pure theory of planning, then, has the task of providing conceptual categories with which we can formally articulate those particular portions of the state and the market whose elements are to be found in every effective plan. These categories, we shall find, are already available to us in Kelsen's jurisprudence and Walras' economics. The way in which they are to be co-ordinated, however, poses problems which require careful consideration.

CHAPTER IV

Efficacy and Value in Plans

Order is Heaven's first law ...
Alexander Pope[1]

AN unplanned society—if, indeed, such a vagary were possible in the real world—would be an unfree society. An unplanned society would be one devoid of the norms which prescribe what ought to be or has a right to be at any future time. Its only propositions would be sentences which predict whatever is going to be (or which describe whatever is or has been).

In such an order, of course, human agents would be no more than the passive instruments of activities which had been predicted by the sentences constituting that order. For such agents there could be no option between the "will be," on the one hand, and the "ought to be" or the "having a right to be," on the other hand. Such agents would be unfree. For it is only through planning that human agents achieve their freedom. It is only in plans whose present normative content corresponds to the future empirical content of a natural order that freedom accrues to human agents. Yet such normative content, we know, does not in any way *predict* the future empirical content of the natural order; it

---

[1] Alexander Pope, "An Essay on Man," in *The Augustans*, edited by Maynard Mack (Englewood Cliffs, N.J.: Prentice-Hall, Inc., 1950), p. 302.

can only state what that content ought to be or has a right to be. Freedom, in other words, presupposes a plan which works but which might not have worked.

The Concept of Value

Now how are we going to interpret this relationship between the prescriptions of a plan and the predictions of a science? How are we going to relate the art of planning to the science of planning—particularly in view of our previous observation that no plan can be valid unless it is first effective—unless, that is to say, its normative content does in some measure correspond to future reality? These questions pose anew the problem of conceptualizing the relationship between two distinct orders of phenomena: the natural and the normative.

The natural order, of course, is the domain of science, just as the normative order is the domain of art. Both are epistemological constructions by which the human mind perceives and organizes events—in the one case, events that can be judged as true or false by an appeal to experience, in the other case, events that can be judged as valid or invalid by an appeal to norms.

The natural order finds its description in scientific laws which specify invariant relationships of dependency among the events of experience and which thereby predict future relationships among those events. The natural order is a given for all normative judgments; it is, so to speak, real.

The normative order, for its part, finds its expression in propositions that prescribe which events ought to occur or have a right to occur. Such events may or may not correspond in content to the events of the natural order. If they happen to correspond perfectly, the normative order becomes redundant to the natural order and can have little interest in its own right. If the events do not correspond at all, the normative order is not an effective one. Between these two extremes lie the interesting cases in which the events prescribed or permitted by the normative order correspond in a general way to those predicted by the natural order, but with just enough discrepancy to allow some option to the human agent —from which fact the human agent derives his freedom. Such a normative order is an effective order.

Now, in all strictness, when we say that a normative order is an effective order we are really referring, in an elliptical way, to an attribute of the natural order. Norms *per se* can be neither effective nor ineffective; it is only their behavioral and psychological counterparts, which are part of natural reality, that can be effective or ineffective. Efficacy, in other words, is a matter of the "is" rather than of the "ought to be" or the "having a right to be." What, then, can be the attribute of a normative order which is correlative to its efficacy—that is, correlative to its realization in behavioral and psychological reality? That attribute is not *validity*, for the validity of a norm presupposes some additional conditions, over and above the efficacy of the order to which it belongs, namely, the absence of contradiction with other norms, and its enactment in a way that has been prescribed by the basic norm.[2] Clearly we are going to have to posit some additional attribute of the normative order—one which is, for the realm of the "ought to be" or the "having a right to be," correlative to the efficacy of that order in the realm of the "is."

For this purpose the concept of *value* recommends itself. By this term we shall mean any directive which proceeds from a higher norm to the lower norms of an order.[3] A value is a sen-

---

[2] Hans Kelsen, *General Theory of Law and State,* trans. by Anders Wedberg (Cambridge, Massachusetts: Harvard University Press, 1945), pp. 113, 401–407.

[3] In this definition of *value* we depart from both Kelsen and Walras, basing ourselves rather on the analysis of Clyde Kluckhohn and others in "Values and Value-Orientations in the Theory of Action," in Talcott Parsons and Edward A. Shils, *Toward a General Theory of Action* (Cambridge, Massachusetts: Harvard University Press, 1951), pp. 388–433.

tence which states just which activities a lower norm ought to prescribe or permit. Such a sentence might be the following: "The
statutes of a democracy ought to stipulate some equalization in the
distribution of wealth." In its predicate form value becomes an
attribute which attaches to an activity through the enjoining of
that activity by a higher norm to the lower norms of an order.
Thus the value of "equalization in the distribution of wealth"
might attach to such activities as collective bargaining and the
maintenance of full employment. Value likewise attaches as a
predicate to the lower norms which have "accepted" the in-
junction of a higher norm and which duly prescribe or permit the
enjoined activity.

Let us proceed, then, to an examination of the concept of value,
regarding it as the unique attribute of a normative order (and of
the activities specified by that order) which corresponds to the
efficacy of that order in behavioral and psychological reality. In
our approach to the concept of value we are going to rely once
again on Kelsen's device of the basic norm, adapting it, however,
to a somewhat different purpose. Just as the basic norm allowed
us to determine whether or not an activity which is prescribed or
permitted by a norm has *validity*, so the same device, or a very
similar one, should allow us to determine whether or not an activity which is prescribed or permitted by a norm has *value*. The
basic norm, of course, is a proposition whose antecedent clause
hypothesizes the possible occurrence of one kind of activity, and
whose consequent clause prescribes or permits a contrary kind of
activity. In this respect the basic norm states a relationship between a contingent set of activities in the natural realm and a consequent set of activities in the normative realm. To be sure, the
contingent activities of the antecedent clause do have an implied
normative status—a point of view which has governed most of
our analysis up to this point. Yet strictly speaking the normative-
ness of the antecedent clause is only epiphenomenal to the norma-

tiveness of the consequent clause.[4] Basically the antecedent clause of a norm is a hypothesis concerning the natural realm, whereas the consequent clause of a norm is a prescription or permission concerning the normative realm. When we say: "If the management of the southern branch of The Allied Units Trust does not maintain an annual increase in production of five percent over the next six years, then the directors of that trust ought to remove the management," we are indeed implying that the management of the southern branch *ought* to maintain the indicated rate of increase in production. Such an ought, however, is but the contrapositive of the ought which was expressed in the original statement. Basically the antecedent clause of the statement hypothesizes a possible event in the natural realm, namely, a failure to maintain a stated rate of increase in production, and it links to this hypothetical event in the natural realm a conditional consequent in the normative realm, namely, a prescription that the management ought to be removed.

So it is with the basic legal norm and the basic economic norm. Consider the two if-clauses: *If the command of a supreme authority be violated,* . . . and *If means are offered to an individual which are not those he is asking for,* . . . Each of these clauses hypothesizes a possible activity in the natural realm of behavioral events. Consider now the two corresponding then-clauses: . . . *then coercive sanctions ought to be applied by that authority,* and . . . *then that individual has a right to either accept or reject the offer with a view to organizing his own complement of means into activities which will maximize his utility.* One of these then-clauses specifies an activity which ought to occur; the other specifies an activity which has a right to occur. Where the two if-clauses pertain to the natural realm, the two then-clauses pertain to the normative realm.

[4] Kelsen, *Law and State*, pp. 60–61.

The Mediate Norm

Let us now apply this device to the concept of value. We shall begin by constructing what we may call the *mediate norm*—a presupposition which must answer to the same epistemological criteria as Kelsen's basic legal norm and the cognate basic economic norm. Just as the two basic norms allowed us to judge norms, and the activities stipulated by those norms, as having or not having validity, so the mediate norm must allow us to judge norms, and the activities stipulated by those norms, as having or not having value. Likewise, where the two basic norms found their justification in the degree of correspondence which they afforded between the content of activities defined by them as valid in a normative order and the content of activities which actually occur in the natural order, so the mediate norm must find its justification in the degree of correspondence which it affords between the formal measure of value which it attaches to an activity, viewed as part of the normative order, and the contribution which that activity makes to the efficacy of its order in human behavior. By the term *contribution* here we refer to the degree of dependency, with respect to the attribute of want-gratification and want-deprivation, which obtains between a given activity and any or all of the remaining activities that comprise a natural order of behavior.[5] We must, then, choose as our mediate norm that one proposition

[5] In thus granting parametric status to the attribute of want-gratification and want-deprivation we are in no way denying the enormous variability in cultural content which each "position" on this attribute can have as between different societies and historical periods. We are, however, treating want-gratification and want-deprivation as an *a priori* psychological dimension which may be imposed by the pure theorist upon any defined class of human activities in a way that will permit the formulation of meaningful propositions about those activities. Cf. Talcott Parsons, *The Social System* (New York: The Free Press of Glencoe, Inc., 1951), Chapter I, and p. 352.

which will maximize the correspondence between value as a normative datum and efficacy as a natural datum. Like the two basic norms, of course, the mediate norm is an untestable hypothesis. It is an entirely formal construction. Its purpose is to serve as a "standard of valuation"[6] by means of which we can decide whether or not a given activity ought to be part of a plan or has a right to be such a part.

The proposition which would seem to answer most fully to these criteria can be stated as follows: *If and only if there is an activity which lies outside the set of activities that constitute a natural order of human behavior, then and only then that activity should not be prescribed or permitted by any norms which have their focus in an individual and/or in the supreme authority.* In this statement the antecedent clause refers to a hypothetical situation in natural reality which would violate the conditions of efficacy of a normative order. The consequent clause is a directive which states that such a situation should not be prescribed or permitted by any of the norms of an order. Let us examine each of these clauses in the order indicated.

The first clause presupposes the availability of a scientific theory of human behavior. The postulates and theorems which would comprise such a theory—that is, the scientific laws—set limits to the variety of activities that will comport with a natural order of human events, and these limits correspond to the ones that are normally given in experience. A natural order, then, is an artifact of a scientific theory. But more than this, it is a probability sample of experience. It is a set of probable conditions with which every normative order must comply if the activities that it prescribes or permits are to be valid. According to the antecedent clause of the mediate norm a certain class of hypothetical activities are not normally to be found in experience. The contribution

6 Kelsen, *Law and State*, p. 41.

which such activities make to the efficacy of a normative order is indiscernible; they can not, therefore, be regarded as part of the natural order. This class of hypothetical activities represents the logical complement of the class of activities which normally occur in experience and which as such are part of the natural order. The antecedent clause of the mediate norm really amounts to the hypothesis that certain activities might occur in reality which are not part of the natural order (though they would be part of the natural realm of events).

When we turn from the antecedent clause to the consequent clause we move from the natural to the normative realm. The link between the two is a material equivalence, reflecting our agnosticism concerning the metaphysical status of the relationship between the natural and the normative; the equivalence *per se* adds nothing to our knowledge of the consequent clause beyond what we already knew or posited of it. The mediate norm, therefore, comports with either a naturalist or an intuitionist theory of value. The consequent clause of this mediate norm imputes nonvalue to any activity whose composition of means and ends places it outside the set of activities which constitute a natural order; it directs that no lesser norm shall prescribe or permit such activities. To all other activities it imputes value, directing that lesser norms shall prescribe or permit such activities.

Value, then, becomes that unique attribute of an activity (whose content forms part of a normative order) which corresponds to the contribution made by that activity (whose content forms part of a natural order as well) to the efficacy of its normative order. As such it becomes a necessary (though not necessary and sufficient) condition of the validity of an activity. From this perspective it is possible to appreciate the true import of Jellinek's concept of the *normative Kraft des Faktischen*:[7] what is not fac-

---

[7] Georg Jellinek, *Allgemeine Staatslehre* (Berlin: O. Häring, 1900), pp. 307–310.

tual cannot have value, and what does not have value cannot have validity.

The *modus operandi* by which value gets ascribed to an activity is similar to that by which validity is ascribed. Value ascription, that is to say, is specified in the mediate norm as the prerogative of every individual and of the supreme authority. They are the ones who are authorized to determine, by their continual "testing of reality," whether an activity has value. Discrete individuals, for instance, are authorized to assign value to an activity by so pricing the various factors and products which are involved in that activity as to equate supply and demand for each of those commodities. Similarly the supreme authority, or a duly constituted representative thereof, is authorized to assign value to an activity by promulgating statutes, interpretations, or rulings about it.

The mediate norm, and the concept of value which it defines, is to be our device for coordinating the empirical events of a natural order with the prescribed or permitted events of a plan as a normative order. By means of the mediate norm we shall be able to determine, in a formal way, just which activities comport with an effective plan. By means of the mediate norm we shall be able to fix the limits of obedience and the limits of rationality in any effective plan. By means of it, finally, we shall bridge the gap between the science of planning, which predicts, and the art of planning, which prescribes and permits.

To realize the full analytic power of the mediate norm we shall find it helpful to make one refinement in the form of its statement. We shall assume that the mediate norm consists of a whole series of antecedent clauses each member of which, by hypothesis, implies one member of a whole series of consequent clauses. In this refinement the members of each of the two series of clauses are arranged according to magnitude. In the first series—the series of antecedent clauses—the member clauses are arranged according to the magnitude of the contribution which each of the activities specified by them makes to the efficacy of its normative order in human behavior, that is, according to the degree of dependency[8] which obtains, with respect to the attribute of want-gratification, between each such activity and any or all of the remaining activities in its order. In the second series—the series of consequent clauses—the member clauses are arranged according to the urgency with which an activity is supposed to be invested by the lower norms of the order that is constituted by those clauses, that is, according to the extremity of the sanctions which are supposed to be prescribed or permitted by the lower norms of the order in case the aforesaid activity should not occur. The assumption is that an activity which would make a lesser contribution to the efficacy of its order *should* be invested with lesser urgency by the lower norms of that order. Hence, where the mediate norm might have been very generally rendered as follows:

(1) *If and only if an activity* x *is outside the natural order of human behavior* $\mathcal{B}$, *then and only then* x *should be outside the normative order* $\mathcal{V}$,

it can now be rendered in these terms:

(2) *If and only if* x *is outside* B_n, *then and only then* x *should be outside* V_n,
If and only if x *is outside* B_{n-1}, *then and only then* x *should be outside* V_{n-1},

. . . .

If and only if x *is outside* B_1, *then and only then* x *should be outside* V_1.

In these graduated variants of the mediate norm, B_n represents

---

[8] Among the parameters involved in each such "degree of dependency" are the production coefficients of input-output analysis. A production coefficient indicates how much commodity output of one activity goes as a factor into the production of one unit of commodity output of another activity.

the subset of activities of the natural order $\mathcal{B}$ whose contributions to the efficacy of their order would be maximal; V_n represents the subset of activities of the normative order $\mathcal{V}$ which are supposed to be invested with maximal urgency by the norms of that order. B_1 and V_1 represent the corresponding minimal subsets of $\mathcal{B}$ and $\mathcal{V}$, respectively. Each of the consequent clauses in this series is a directive to the lower norms of its order, enjoining them to prescribe or permit specified activities at given degrees of urgency. Every such clause *is* a value, and each of the enjoined activities *has* a value.

This refinement of the mediate norm presupposes, of course, that for the set $\mathcal{B}$ of activities in the natural realm we have some measure of the magnitude of every subset B_i, B_j in $\mathcal{B}$ such that if $B_i < B_j$ then the measure of B_i is less than the measure of B_j. Likewise it presupposes that for the set $\mathcal{V}$ of activities in the normative realm we have some measure of the magnitude of every subset V_i, V_j in $\mathcal{V}$ such that if $V_i < V_j$ then the measure of V_i is less than the measure of V_j.

With this refinement in the mediate norm it becomes possible to compare activities in respect to their value, locating them within one or another subset of $\mathcal{V}$ according to the measure of urgency with which they are supposed to be invested by the norms of their order. Since, by hypothesis, each magnitude of value as specified in one of the consequent clauses of the mediate norm corresponds to one and only one degree of dependency as specified in an antecedent clause of that norm, it follows that the value of an activity becomes a surrogate, in the normative order, of the empirical conditions under which that order can be realized in behavior. In other words we may use value as a summary indicator of the conditions which a normative order must meet if it is to be effective—if, that is to say, the activities which it prescribes or permits are to conform with a natural order. Activities must have at least a minimum degree of value if the normative order to which they belong can be effective and if the norms which prescribe them are to be valid. In this fact we discover the real import of the mediate norm.

The Dual Source of the Validity of Plan Norms

To appreciate its full significance let us return to the problem with which we closed our previous chapter. There we suggested, quite provisionally, that a plan is a normative order which overlaps, in a way that has yet to be determined, with two other normative orders: the state and the market. The focus of one of these orders is the collectivity having an obligation to enforce obedience; the focus of the other is the individual having a right to be rational. Each of these orders is confronted by limits beyond which it cannot be effective; each is confronted by facts of which its basic norm fails to take account. How are we to determine these limits? How can we identify the particular portions of the state and the market which are to be found in every effective plan? The answers to these questions have been put within our reach by the device of the mediate norm.

To begin with, it is possible that the prescriptions of the state will, at many points, differ from the permissions of the market. There is nothing in the basic legal norm nor in the basic economic norm that would guarantee the mutual consistency of all the lesser norms which owe their validity to two such different basic norms. The state and the market, then, so far as they are regarded as sets of valid norms, do not admit of a one-to-one transformation from one to the other; they are not identical with their overlap.

At the same time, however, as indicated in the preceding chapter, the assumption of some overlap is imposed upon our thought by the phenomenon of the contract. Likewise in the norms of a plan we are led to the same assumption of a conjunction between prescriptions of the state and permissions of the market. In this conjunction every activity of a plan finds itself, at one and the same time, sanctioned by a law as well as by a price (though the law may at times be determinable only through adjudication, and the price may be only a "shadow price"[9]). The prototypical plan norm, joining together the "ought to be" and the "having a right to be," would read as follows:

"If any one of a designated class of individuals does not observe a specified activity, then:

the government ought to apply coercive measures to the wayward individual,
&
other individuals have a right to restrict the range of alternative means which would otherwise be available to that individual."

We have, therefore, the task of formulating conceptual categories for a class of norms whose validity is conditional on the efficacy of *two* other orders rather than on that of only one. Since, then, the norms of different orders can be simultaneously valid only if those orders have in some way been coordinated (so as to exclude the possibility of contradictory norms), it follows that the state and the market cannot be entirely disjoint. There must, in other words, be some attribute of these two orders in terms of which they overlap. That attribute has been given us by the mediate norm. It is the attribute of value. By the simple expedient of arranging activities according to their value we shall be able to identify those portions of the state and of the market which are common to both and which, therefore, represent a link between the two. In this way we shall find it possible to view a plan as a unified normative order even though it has been constructed out of two rather different normative orders.

In arranging activities according to their value it is helpful to visualize them as elements located within one (or both) of two sets of concentric rings. Each such ring is a subset within a set of

---

[9] J. R. Hicks, *Value and Capital* (London: Oxford University Press, 1946), pp. 110–111.

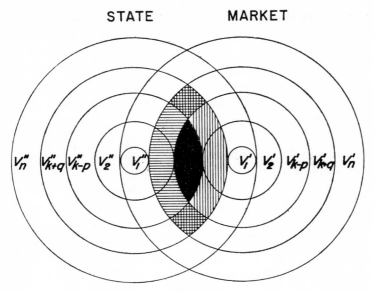

STATE   MARKET

FIGURE 2

rings. One such set corresponds to the state; the other corresponds to the market. Within each of these sets the subsets, or concentric rings, are arranged according to the value which attaches to their component activities. Thus in Figure 2 the innermost pair of subsets contains those activities whose value is minimal: V''_1 for the state, V'_1 for the market. The next outlying pair of subsets— a pair of encircling rings, as it were—contains activities whose value is somewhat greater: V''_2 for the state, V'_2 for the market. The outermost pair of subsets or rings is comprised of those activities whose value is maximal: V''_n for the state, V'_n for the market.

We have hypothesized, now, that these two sets of rings—the state and the market—are not disjoint; there is some degree of overlap between them (see Figure 2). The form of this relationship can be represented as an intersection or logical product. Let $\mathcal{V}''$ denote the set of subsets (rings) which comprise the state, and $\mathcal{V}'$ the set of subsets (rings) which comprise the market. Any overlap between these two sets can be represented as an intersection of the form: $\mathcal{V}''\cdot\mathcal{V}'$. Such an intersection means that there are activities prescribed by the laws of the state that have been simultaneously permitted by the prices of the market, and vice versa. It does not mean, however, that all of these are going to be effective.

In such simultaneously prescribed and permitted activities, whatever is obligatory becomes right, and whatever is right becomes obligatory. More precisely, in any overlap between the state and the market, the right of an individual to be rational is predicated on the obligation of the supreme authority to prevent others from obstructing that individual's rationality. So too, the obligation of an individual to obey the supreme authority presupposes the right of other individuals to be rational. This complementarity of rights and obligations is characteristic of every valid plan viewed as an overlap between the state and the market.

It can be postulated, now, that if a subset of activities V''_i (a ring) of the state does not overlap with a subset V'_j (a ring) of the market, in the sense just indicated, then there will be no overlap between any of the smaller rings of those two systems—for example, between the subsets V''_{i-1} of the state and V'_{j-1} of the market, both of whose activities have less value than the first two subsets. In algebraic form, if $V''_i\cdot V'_j = 0$ for some particular $i, j \leqslant n$, then $V''_{i-1}\cdot V'_{j-1} = 0$. The assumption is that if the state and the market do not jointly specify activities which have a given value they will not jointly specify activities which have lesser value.

Further, some empirical boundary conditions can be postulated for $\mathcal{V}'''$ and $\mathcal{V}'$, such that V''_{k-p} (where $[k - p] > 1$) is the smallest subset of $\mathcal{V}'''$, having an overlap with $\mathcal{V}'$, whose elements will comport with an effective market, and such that $\mathcal{V}'_{k-p}$ is the smallest subset of $\mathcal{V}'$, having an overlap with $\mathcal{V}'''$, whose elements will comport with an effective state.[10] The first of these conditions states that there is a minimum overlap of the state with the market below which activities prescribed by the state are incompatible with the market. The second of the conditions states that there is a minimum overlap of the market with the state below which activities permitted by the market are incompatible with the state. The intersection $V''_{k-p} \cdot V'_{k-p}$ of the two subsets represents a minimal overlap of activities that can be simultaneously effective for the state and the market.

Further boundary conditions can be postulated so that V''_{k+q} (where $[k+q] < n$) is the largest subset of $\mathcal{V}''$, having an overlap with $\mathcal{V}'$, whose elements will comport with an effective market, and such that V'_{k+q} is the largest subset of $\mathcal{V}'$, having an overlap with $\mathcal{V}''$, whose elements will comport with an effective state. The first of these conditions states that there is a maximum overlap of the state with the market, above which activities prescribed by the state are incompatible with the market. The second of the conditions states that there is a maximum overlap of the market with the state above which activities permitted by the market are incompatible with the state. The intersection $V''_{k+q} \cdot V'_{k+q}$ of the two subsets represents a maximal overlap of activities that can be simultaneously effective for the state and the market. Together these boundary conditions formulate the lower and upper limits for the coexistence of the state and the market as effective normative orders. Empirical considerations to be adduced in the following chapter will lead us to a still further constriction, within these limits, of the range of subsets that can in fact be simultaneously effective for the state and the market.

We are now in a position to define the various types of intersections that are formally conceivable between subsets of activities

---

[10] The letters k, p and q represent fixed indexes whose referents will be defined in the chapter which follows.

prescribed by the state and subsets of activities permitted by the
market. There are five pairs of possibilities:

(i) $V''_{k-p} \cdot V'_{k-p} < E$ (i)′ $V''_{k+q} \cdot V'_{k+q} < E$

(ii) $V''_{k-p} \cdot V'_{k-(p-1)} < E$ (ii)′ $V''_{k+q} \cdot V'_{k+(q+1)} \nless E$

(iii) $V''_{k-p} \cdot V'_{k-(p+1)} \nless E$ (iii)′ $V''_{k+q} \cdot V'_{k+(q-1)} < E$

(iv) $V''_{k-(p-1)} \cdot V'_{k-p} < E$ (iv)′ $V''_{k+(q+1)} \cdot V'_{k+q} \nless E$

(v) $V''_{k-(p+1)} \cdot V'_{k-p} \nless E$ (v)′ $V''_{k+(q-1)} \cdot V'_{k+q} < E$

where $[k - p] > 1$ and $[k + q] < n$, (k, p and q being fixed indexes); and where E is the set of activities that can be simultaneously effective for both the state and the market.

Of these five pairs of possibilities, the intersection $V''_{k-p} \cdot V'_{k-p}$ represents a minimal overlap of all the subsets V''_i and V'_j. That is to say, it is the smallest subset in which there are activities that can be simultaneously and effectively prescribed by the state and permitted by the market. It is, so to speak, the minimal intersection between the state and the market. Likewise the intersection $V''_{k+q} \cdot V'_{k+q}$ represents a maximal overlap of all the subsets V''_i and V'_j. It is the largest subset in which there are activities that can be simultaneously and effectively prescribed by the state and permitted by the market. Activities whose value puts them below or above these minimal or maximal intersections cannot be part of an effective plan. Such activities might have validity in the state or in the market, but not in both. The activities of a plan, on the other hand, constituted as it is of both of these normative orders, can only be valid if those activities have no less than the value which is represented by the minimal intersection of subsets from the two sets V'' and V', and no more than the value which is represented by the maximal intersection of subsets from those two sets.

Activities which occupy the other eight types of intersections [(ii)−(v) and (ii)′−(v)′] are all characterized by an asymmetry, relative to value, as between the prescriptions of the state and the permissions of the market. The intersection $V''_{k-p} \cdot V'_{k-(p+1)}$, for example, is composed of activities whose value for the state is somewhat greater than their value for the market. Such activities are supposed to be invested with greater urgency by the laws of the state than by the prices of the market; that is, the sanctions which are supposed to be prescribed by law, in case the specified activities fail to occur, are more extreme than those which are supposed to be permitted by prices. In all such asymmetries the right of an individual to be rational in the market either exceeds or falls short of other individuals' obligations to obey the supreme authority in protecting that individual's rationality. The behavioral significance of such asymmetries will be considered in some detail in Chapter VI.

Intersections $V''_{k-p} \cdot V'_{k-p}$ and $V''_{k+q} \cdot V'_{k+q}$, then, represent the lower and upper limits between which the activities of every valid plan must lie. These limits, to be sure, can have no more than a formal character. They are artifacts of our mediate norm and of our assumption that planning has a dual source of validity in both the state and the market. It was, of course, the mediate norm which allowed us in the first place to link the natural order with the normative order via the conceptual category of *value*. And it was the category of *value* which allowed us to view a plan as a unified suborder even though it be constructed out of two such distinct normative orders as the state and the market. In performing these functions the mediate norm has offered us the possibility of a pure theory of planning in terms of which human agents, though comprising part of a determined and determining natural order, may nevertheless be free. Before we elaborate on this point, however, let us examine a little more closely the formal structure of value, with a view now to determining the precise location of a valid plan within the overlap of the state and the market.

CHAPTER V

The Structure of Value in Plans

> *But still 'tmust not be thought that in
> all ways
> All things can be conjoined . . .*
>
> Lucretius[1]

THE ELEMENTS of a plan fall into two classes: laws and prices
(along with the activities that are specified therein). Not
every law nor every price, however, can be a valid part of a plan;
the activities which any one of them specifies must not fall above
or below certain maximum and minimum values. Yet a knowledge of what has thus been excluded from a plan can carry us
only a short way toward learning what *must* be included in it.
A plan, after all, is something more than a residual collection of
nonexcluded norms (with the activities specified therein); a plan
must have some structure, some *principium unitatis,* by which it
acquires just those norms which will comport with a valid order.

In looking for this principle we should remind ourselves that
our purpose all along has been to develop the conceptual categories for a pure theory of plannning. Our aim has been to devise
categories which will allow for the whole range of logically conceivable combinations of laws and prices that might *a priori* char-

---

[1] Lucretius, *Of the Nature of Things,* trans. by William Ellery Leonard
(New York: E. P. Dutton and Co., Inc., 1943), Everyman's Library,
Book II, p. 70.

acterize a valid plan. We have not, in other words, confined our attention to the empirically given combinations of laws and prices which happen to characterize the plans that are known to history.

The problem before us, then, is to determine whether or not we have, in the mediate norm, an adequate device for viewing a plan as a unified set of laws and prices. The mediate norm has already enabled us to define two classes of activities which *cannot* be part of an effective plan, namely, those which lie beyond the minimal intersection of the state and the market and those which lie beyond the maximal intersection. Will it now enable us to determine subsets of activities which *must* be part of every effective plan? Can it define additional intersections between the state and the market which will represent activities that must be jointly specified by the laws and the prices of any plan that would be effective? If it can do this then it will have indeed given us the *principium unitatis* by which we may determine which activities have a valid place within a plan and which activities do not.

Possible Combinations of Value in Planning

The answer to these questions has been anticipated in Chapter III. Toward the end of that chapter it was noted that a contract and a governmental plan are alike in one important respect—each of them owes its validity to *both* of the two basic norms: the basic legal norm and the basic economic norm. Each of them expresses the right to be rational and each of them expresses the duty to obey a supreme authority. Upon the signing of a contract there is a dual normative principle: the "right to be" and the "ought to be." A governmental plan, on the other hand, begins with a single normative principle: the "ought to be." In both cases, though, a recognition that objective circumstances may change with the passing of time is always present: contractual terms of exchange which were initially equilibrative may later become disequilibrative; governmentally decreed terms of exchange which were initially disequilibrative may later become equilibrative. In both cases the activities that are involved retain some normative status. The activities stipulated by a contract continue to be valid in terms of the basic legal norm; as such they are supposed to be enforced by the state. The activities stipulated by a governmental plan become valid in terms of the basic economic norm as well as the basic legal norm; as such they acquire a valid place in the market as well as in the state.

This dual filiation of the contract and the governmental plan from two basic norms means that the activities which any of them stipulates will have a valid place, over time, in two normative orders. It means, too, the possibility of additional intersections between the state and the market which lie between the minimal and maximal intersections we have already defined. For to sustain the idea that the activities of a contract—and, likewise, of a governmental plan—can be *valid* in both the state and the market, we have first to assume that those activities have some simultaneous measure of *value* in both the state and the market. Validity, after all, presupposes value. Hence we could only say of contracts and governmental plans that they have validity in two normative orders if we are willing to assume that there are intersections between those two orders—that is, subsets of activities having simultaneous value in both orders. Indeed, we are obliged to allow for the possibility of many such intersections. Specifically, there can be as many intersections as there are different combinations of value magnitudes when all the possible magnitudes for the state are pairwise combined with all of those for the market. It is, of course, the mediate norm which has given us the epistemological basis for defining such intersections between state and market and which thus makes sense of the dual affiliation of contracts and governmental plans with two distinct normative orders.

Yet not all the intersections between state and market will comport with effective planning. There are laws of the natural order which put empirical restrictions upon the combinations of value magnitudes that are otherwise logically possible. A plan can be effective only if it prescribes or permits just those activities which fall within a limited segment of the range of conceivable activities. Therefore, if we are to reach our objective of identifying the types of activities which are characteristic of effective plans we shall have to specify some limits to the correspondence which we have defined between: (1) the various pairwise combinations of value magnitudes which are logically possible between the state and the market, and (2) the dependency relations which obtain among the activities that comprise a natural order of human behavior. Are there certain pairwise combinations of value magnitudes which characterize all plans whose present normative content corresponds to the future empirical content of a natural order? Are there certain dependency relations among activities which never present themselves to observation and whose surrogates in the normative order must therefore be invalid? Is there some distinctive structure which characterizes the activities of all effective plans?

In our approach to this problem we shall find it helpful to consider value as a normative space that is comprised of two dimensions, $\mathcal{V}''$ and $\mathcal{V}'$, with respect to which activities are partially ordered. This view has been implicit in our representation of the state and the market as sets of concentric rings in which each ring is a subset of some prescribed or permitted activities, and in which every overlap of two rings from different sets is an intersection of activities jointly prescribed by the state and permitted by the market. In our diagram (Figure 2) activities which comprise the intersection $V''_{k+q}V'_{k+q}$ are of greater value than those comprising the intersection $V''_{k+q} \cdot V'_{k-p}$, as seen in the relative sizes of those two overlaps. But activities in the intersection $V''_{k+q} \cdot V'_{k-p}$ are neither greater than, nor less than, nor equal to those in $V''_{k-p} \cdot V'_{k+q}$; the two intersections are simply incomparable relative to value, one being greater in value for the state, the other being greater in value for the market. The relationship between pairs of activities from two such intersections forms a partial order rather than a complete order.

For the fullest development of this approach to value we are going to turn to a branch of mathematics known as lattice theory.[2] We shall begin by considering the entire system of intersections of the form $V''_i \cdot V'_j$ (where $i, j \geqslant k - p, i, j \leqslant k + q$) as a system of types of activities, each type $(V''_i \cdot V'_j)$ being an intersection between the state V''' and the market V'. Allowing for all possible pairwise combinations of value magnitudes V'''_i from V''' with V'_j from V', there will be $[(k + q) - (k - p) + 1]^2$ such types of activities. This system of types of activities constitutes a complemented, distributive lattice (a Boolean algebra) in which the elements are the types themselves—including the unions (logical sums) and the intersections (logical products) of those types—and in which every pair of types has a union and an intersection. In this lattice any type of activities which stands higher in value than another type of activities is represented diagrammatically as a point connected by a descending line to the lower activity or point. Thus a vertical chain of points, all connected by a single line, represents a series of types of activities arranged according to ascending and descending value. Types of activities which cannot be compared in respect to value, one being higher on V''' and the other being higher on V', are represented as points between which there is no connecting line. Such types are incomparable with respect to value. $V''_{k+q} \cdot V'_{k+q}$, the maximal intersection between the state and the market, represents the all-element of the lattice; its component activities are higher in value than those of any other type. The minimal intersection between the state and the market, $V''_{k-p} \cdot V'_{k-p}$, is the zero-element of the lattice; its component activities are lower in value than those of any other type.

[2] Garrett Birkhoff, *Lattice Theory*, rev. ed. (New York: American Mathematical Society, 1948).

The lattice provides a system for algebraically manipulating the elements of a partially ordered set. The operations of logical product (·) and logical sum (∨) allow the expression of one type of activity as an isotone function of other types of activities. They further allow the postulation of restrictions on the range of variation which may obtain between the V''_i and V'_j components of any type of activity that would comprise part of an effective plan. As will be indicated presently, not all of the intersections $V''_i \cdot V'_j$ contain valid activities, even though they happen to lie between the minimal and the maximal intersections $V''_{k-p} \cdot V'_{k-p}$ and $V''_{k+q} \cdot V'_{k+q}$. Lattice theory thus offers a model which allows identification of just which of the logically conceivable combinations of laws and prices have the validity that is requisite for a unified plan.

Types of Planning

The lattice which is diagrammed in Figure 3 indicates these relationships. The following analysis will be primarily concerned with identifying which of the various types of activities represented on this lattice may have validity within a plan. Inspection of the diagram will reveal nine classes of types of activities:

1) Types of activities whose two component value magnitudes are equal in both the state and the market. Such activities are supposed to be invested with equal urgency by the laws and the prices of these respective orders, in the sense that the sanctions invoked by these norms are of equal extremity in the event that the prescribed or permitted activities do not occur. In Figure 3 this class is represented by seven intersections, or types of activities, ranging from the zero-element $V''_{k-p} \cdot V'_{k-p}$ at the bottom of the lattice to the all-element $V''_{k+q} \cdot V'_{k+q}$ at the top of the lattice. As such it comprises what will be called here *stability* types of activities and *stability* planning.

2) Types of activities whose value in the market exceeds their value in the state, but neither of whose two component value

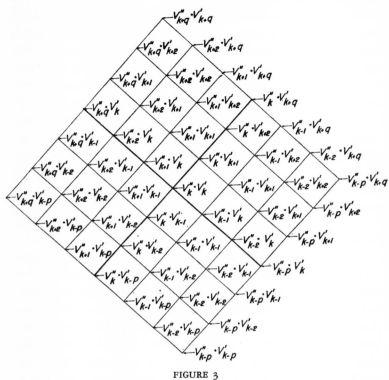

FIGURE 3

magnitudes falls below the value that characterizes a given stability type of activity. Such activities are supposed to be invested
with greater urgency by the prices which permit them than by the
laws which prescribe them, and neither of the sanctions that apply
if the stipulated activities fail to occur has less extremity than
those which apply to a given stability type of activity. In Figure 3
this class is represented by the intersections which extend to the
upper right from any one of the seven stability elements, for
example, $V''_k \cdot V'_k$, comprising in this instance $V''_k \cdot V'_{k+1}$,
$V''_k \cdot V'_{k+2}$, and $V''_k \cdot V'_{k+q}$ (more generally, $V''_k \cdot V'_{i>k}$). It
represents what is called here *individual developmental* plan-
ning.

3) Types of activities whose value in the state exceeds their value in the market, but neither of whose two component value magnitudes falls below the value that characterizes a given stability type of activity. Such activities are supposed to be invested with greater urgency by the laws which prescribe them than by the prices which permit them, and neither of the sanctions that apply if the stipulated activities fail to occur has less extremity than those which apply to a given stability type of activity. In Figure 3 this class is represented by the intersections which extend to the upper left from any one of the seven stability elements, for example again, $V''_k \cdot V'_k$, comprising in this instance $V''_{k+1} \cdot V'_k$, $V''_{k+2} \cdot V'_k$, and $V''_{k+q} \cdot V'_k$ (more generally, $V''_{j>k} \cdot V'_k$). It represents what will be called here *governmental developmental* planning.

4) Types of activities whose value in the market exceeds their value in the state, but neither of whose two component value magnitudes exceeds the value that characterizes a given stability type of activity. Such activities are supposed to be invested with greater urgency by the prices which permit them than by the laws which prescribe them, but neither of the sanctions that apply if the stipulated activities fail to occur has greater extremity than those which apply to a given stability type of activity. In Figure 3 this class is represented by the intersections which extend to the lower right from any one of the seven stability elements, for example again, $V''_k \cdot V'_k$, comprising in this instance $V''_{k-1} \cdot V'_k$, $V''_{k-2} \cdot V'_k$, and $V''_{k-p} \cdot V'_k$ (more generally, $V''_{j<k} \cdot V'_k$). It represents what will be called here *individual allocative* planning.

5) Types of activities whose value in the state exceeds their value in the market, but neither of whose two component value magnitudes exceeds the value that characterizes a given stability type of activity. Such activities are supposed to be invested with greater urgency by the laws which prescribe them than by the prices which permit them, but neither of the sanctions that apply

if the stipulated activities fail to occur have greater extremity than those which apply to a given stability type of activity. In Figure 3 this class is represented by the intersections which extend to the lower left from any one of the seven stability elements, for example again, $V''_k \cdot V'_k$, comprising in this instance $V''_k \cdot V'_{k-1}$, $V''_k \cdot V'_{k-2}$, and $V''_k \cdot V'_{k-p}$ (more generally, $V''_k \cdot V'_{i<k}$). It represents what will be called here *governmental allocative* planning.

6 and 7) Types of activities whose two component value magnitudes are unequal as between the state and the market, with one of the magnitudes exceeding the value that characterizes a given stability type of activity and the other magnitude falling below the value that characterizes that given stability type of activity. Such activities are supposed to be invested with unequal urgency by the laws which prescribe them and the prices which permit them; the sanctions that apply if the stipulated activities fail to occur are *more* extreme in the case of laws and *less* extreme in the case of prices (or vice versa) than those which apply to a given stability type of activity. In Figure 3 this class is represented by the intersections which are situated to the right and the left of any stability element, for example, $V''_k \cdot V'_k$, comprising in this instance all intersections $V''_\alpha \cdot V'_\beta$ and $V''_\beta \cdot V'_\alpha$ (where $\alpha > k$ and $\beta < k$). It represents what will be called here *individual compensatory* planning and *governmental compensatory* planning, depending on whether the *greater* of the two value magnitudes that characterize any particular type of activity happens to be in favor of the market or in favor of the state.

8 and 9) Types of activities whose two component value magnitudes are unequal as between the state and the market but *both* of which magnitudes are either in excess of, or below, the value that characterizes a given stability type of activity. Such activities are supposed to be invested with unequal urgency by the laws which prescribe them and the prices which permit them, in the sense that the sanctions invoked by these norms are of unequal extremity in the event that the stipulated activities do not occur.

In Figure 3 this class is represented by the intersections, or types of activities, which are situated above and below any given stability element, for example, $V''_k \cdot V'_k$ (exclusive of other stability elements), comprising in this instance all intersections $V''_\lambda \cdot V'_\gamma$ (where $\lambda, \gamma > k$ or $\lambda, \gamma < k$, and $\lambda \neq \gamma$). It represents what will be called here *individual structural* planning and *governmental structural* planning, depending on whether the *greater* of the two value magnitudes that characterize any particular type of activity happens to be in favor of the market or in favor of the state.

Now, which of these nine classes of types of activities can be realized in the natural order? Which of them, in respect to their content, ever match the events of experience? Which of them, in short, meet the first requirement of validity, namely, effectiveness? To answer this question we shall turn once again to our epistemological device of the mediate norm; it was, after all, in terms of this device that we first defined the value magnitudes V''_i and V'_j, from which in turn we defined the intersections $V''_i \cdot V'_j$ that form the elements of our lattice of types of activities.

The Sanctions of Plans

The mediate norm, we recall, asserts a correspondence between efficacy as a natural datum and value as a normative datum. According to the mediate norm, if there is any activity x which lies outside the set of activities that constitute a natural order of human behavior, then that activity should not be prescribed or permitted by any norms which have their focus in an individual and/or in the supreme authority. More briefly:

If x is outside $\mathcal{B}$, then x should be outside $\mathcal{V}$,

where $\mathcal{B}$ represents the set of activities which constitute a natural order, and where $\mathcal{V}$ represents the set of activities which constitute a normative order. Refinement of the mediate norm allows us to further specify magnitudes B_i of $\mathcal{B}$ and magnitudes V_i of $\mathcal{V}$, and to then assert a correspondence between such magnitudes.

Finally, consideration of planning as a normative order which overlaps with both the state and the market leads us to define intersections between V''_i for the state and V'_j for the market, yielding the types of activities $V''_i \cdot V'_j$ which form the elements of our lattice. Each such type $V''_i \cdot V'_j$ is defined as a conjunction of two directives, one from the state, the other from the market, each of them enjoining the lower norms of its respective order to prescribe or permit specified activities at stated degrees of urgency. Where $i = j$ these degrees of urgency are equal; where $i \neq j$ they are unequal. In other words, the extremity of the sanctions which are supposed to be prescribed by the lower norms of the state in the event that a specified activity fails to occur may or may not equal the extremity of the sanctions which are supposed to be permitted by the lower norms of the market. Thus $V''_i \cdot V'_j$, where $i < j$, represents a subset of activities which are supposed to be invested with greater urgency by the lower norms of the market than by those of the state; as such the sanctions which permit them are supposed to be more extreme than the sanctions which prescribe them.

What, then, is the empirical counterpart of these directives from the mediate norm? The formulation of this corresponding datum depends upon consideration of certain behavioral characteristics of human beings as subjects of the mediate norm. It requires digression from the analysis of the normative order and an outline of certain features of the natural order.

We have said that the different types of activities which enter into a plan will differ in respect to the extremity of the sanctions which are supposed to be applied in case the relevant activities fail to occur. In this concept of extremity, of course, we have perforce defined an *empirical* relationship between a sanction, considered now as a psychological datum, and a human response, viewed as a behavioral datum. The extremity of a sanction, that is to say, can be gauged only in terms of such naturalistic phenomena as intrapersonality defense and interpersonal adjustment—

basic socio-psychological processes that are universal to all of mankind.[3] From this empirical point of view a sanction is a contingent event which is anticipated *ex ante* by the human subject of a norm in the case that he should fail to perform the activity which is specified by that norm. The extremity of the sanction is, in the first instance, a matter of the consequences—intrapersonal and interpersonal—which that individual anticipates through his nonobservance of the norm in question. Such consequences can range all the way from a disadvantageous market transaction to political exile, including all the intervening extremities represented by demotion, discharge, imprisonment, etc.

In a more fundamental sense, however, the extremity of a sanction consists of a relationship which obtains between: (a) the activities that are prescribed or permitted by the norm of which that sanction is a part, and (b) the stable, persistent expectations which individuals have in regard to want-gratification and want-deprivation (gratification and deprivation being viewed as opposite directions on a single psychological continuum).[4] In this respect it is possible to distinguish three degrees of extremity among the sanctions of various plan norms:

1) overmotivating sanctions
2) motivating sanctions
3) undermotivating sanctions

Overmotivating sanctions are the most extreme. The activities upon whose nonperformance they are contingent impose too much want-deprivation on individuals relative to that which is expected by them. Such activities violate that tenuous balance between gratification and deprivation which must characterize the civilized human being upon whom every effective order is pred-

---

[3] Talcott Parsons, *The Social System* (New York: The Free Press of Glencoe, Inc., 1951), p. 203.
[4] *Ibid.*, p. 352.

icated. To be sure, overmotivating laws do give rise to strict obedience, and overmotivating prices do give rise to strict rationality. But they also give rise to anomalous responses on the part of their human subjects: covert subversion, passive withdrawal, and obsessive behavior. These anomalous responses have consequences for the other activities of an order which violate the conditions of efficacy of that order.

Undermotivating sanctions, on the other hand, lie at the opposite pole of extremity. The activities upon whose nonperformance they are contingent demand less of their human subjects than is expected by those individuals. Undermotivated individuals are indifferently obedient or rational, and they manifest anomalous responses such as duplicity, opportunism, and apathy toward the norms of their order.

Motivating sanctions represent an intermediate degree of extremity. The activities to which they are attached require responses of their human subjects that comport with an expected gratification-deprivation balance such as characterizes the civilized human being. Motivated individuals are moderately rational and they are moderately obedient; they tend to compare alternative combinations of means with a view to increasing the gratification of their wants, and they tend to obey the commands of a supreme authority, thereby incurring only a moderate deprivation of their wants. In the face of contradictions between the two precepts of rationality and obedience they vary the application of these precepts in an *ad hoc* manner from one situation to another. Such individuals represent the *homo ambivalensis* that sustains every effective plan and every effective normative order.

We should now remind ourselves of our immediate problem: we are trying to identify the empirical counterpart to each of the types of activities $V''_i \cdot V'_j$ which form the elements of our lattice. That counterpart we have now identified. It is a type or subset of activities characterized by a pair of sanctions, each of which sanctions has some degree of extremity (from the trichotomy:

overmotivating, motivating, undermotivating), and the two of which have been perceived by their human agents as a contingent event that will occur if any of the activities to which they attach should fail to take place. One of these sanctions is specified by a law, the other is specified by a price; both of them are joined in a plan norm which is viewed now as an element of a natural realm of human behavior.

The correspondence between a type of activities viewed (in respect to content) as a normative datum and a type of activities viewed (in respect to content) as a natural datum can be defined thus:

$$\text{Normative} \qquad\qquad \text{Natural}$$
$$V''_i \cdot V'_j \qquad \longleftrightarrow \qquad (x''_i, x'_j)$$

where the subscripts i and j denote the extremities of the sanctions which apply if a specified activity fails to occur. It is well also to regard these extremities henceforth as continuous variables rather than as trichotomies. Finally, the subscript k now denotes that particular degree of extremity which has been called "motivating." Thus i, j, where i, $j > k$, denote overmotivating sanctions; i, j, where i, $j < k$, denote undermotivating sanctions; and i, j, where i, $j = k$ denote motivating sanctions.

With this identification of the empirical counterpart (x''_i, x'_j) of a given type of activities $V''_i \cdot V'_j$ a fundamental postulate of planning theory can be formulated. Then, on the basis of this postulate, the central problem of this chapter can be reapproached —the problem of determining which types of activities can be realized in a natural order of human behavior. Next, it will be seen that it is from these, and only these, types of activities that a plan must make its selection, for only these types will meet that minimum requirement for the validity of any plan norms, namely, the efficacy of the plan as a whole. A plan whose laws and prices specify just these activities, and no others, will possess unity, and its laws and prices can be valid norms. Finally, it will appear that these attributes could have accrued to a plan only as a consequence of positing the mediate norm as an epistemological construct.

The Limits of Effective Planning

The postulate now to be considered purports to be a universally true empirical proposition concerning the consequences, for the efficacy of a plan, of reliance upon overmotivating sanctions, motivating sanctions, and undermotivating sanctions. The postulate asserts that some reliance upon motivating sanctions is a necessary (though not a necessary and sufficient) condition for the consistency of a plan with any of the possible structures that would comprise a natural order of human behavior. The contrapositive of the postulate asserts that exclusive reliance upon overmotivating or undermotivating sanctions is a sufficient (though not a necessary and sufficient) condition for the nonconsistency of a plan with any of the possible structures that would comprise a natural order of human behavior. The following two universally quantified propositions state the postulate concisely:

1) $(X < \mathcal{B}) \supset (X < \mathcal{X})$
2) $(X < {\sim} \mathcal{X}) \supset (X < {\sim} \mathcal{B})$

In these propositions X denotes the set of activities, comprehending certain subsets (x''_i, x'_j), which activities have been prescribed and permitted by the norms of a given plan. The symbol $\mathcal{X}$ denotes the set of all (x''_i, x'_j) where either or both i, $j = k$; ${\sim} \mathcal{X}$ comprehends all subsets (x''_i, x'_j) where neither i nor $j = k$. The symbol $\mathcal{B}$ denotes the set of activities whose dependency relations with one another, relative to the attribute of want-gratification and want-deprivation, are those that can be observed somewhere in a natural order of human behavior; as such $\mathcal{B}$ denotes a set of possible structures B_i. The symbol ${\sim} \mathcal{B}$ includes those subsets of activities whose dependency relations with one another do not form part of the natural order. (x''_i, x'_j), as before, denotes any subset of activities characterized by the indicated magnitudes of the sanctions which are stipulated, respectively, by a particular law and a particular price, the two of which have been joined together in a plan norm. Implication 1 assumes that at least one of the two sanctions of a particular plan norm is a motivating rather than an over- or undermotivating one. Implication 2 assumes that neither of the two sanctions of a particular plan norm is a motivating rather than an over- or undermotivating one.

Together the two implications assert that the dependency relations which obtain among the activities that constitute a natural order of human behavior are restricted to certain ranges of variation which have been observed and formulated by a science of human behavior. They further assert that these dependency relations only obtain when at least one component of the pair of sanctions which characterizes an activity is a motivating sanction —that is, when either or both $i, j = k$. They imply that the dependency relations will fail to conform with scientific observation and theory if both components of a pair of sanctions are over- or undermotivating sanctions—that is, when neither i nor $j = k$. In short, overly high or overly low extremities in *both* components of a pair of sanctions will not comport with the scientifically established ranges of variation in dependency relations which obtain among the activities that characterize a natural order of human behavior. The invariance relations of such a natural order hold only if some of the laws and some of the prices of that order involve an intermediate degree of extremity in the sanctions which apply when any of the activities in that order fail to occur.

The significance of this postulate for a pure theory of planning is not hard to see. Given the correspondence which we have defined between the content of (x''_i, x'_j) in the natural realm of events and the content of $V''_i \cdot V'_j$ in the normative realm of events, whatever empirical limits apply to the former will apply perforce to the latter. Hence only those activities whose sanctions have extremities that comport with a natural order of human behavior can be valid activities, because only they can meet the first requirement of validity, namely, efficacy.

Certain questions arise when this conclusion is applied to the nine classes of types of activities defined in the analysis of Figure 3. Which of these types of activities could be valid elements in any plan? Which of them would be invalid? The answer to these questions may be reached by a process of elimination of invalid types of activities. When the second implication of the empirical postulate is invoked

$$2)\ \ (X < \sim \mathcal{X}) \supset (X < \sim \mathcal{B}),$$

where $\sim \mathcal{X}$ consists of subsets (x''_i, x'_j) where neither i nor $j = k$, and when the correspondence which we have defined between:

$$V''_i \cdot V'_j \quad \longleftrightarrow \quad (x''_i, x'_j),$$

is recalled, then it becomes clear that all those types of activities $V''_i \cdot V'_j$ where neither i nor $j = k$ will be invalid types of activities. In other words, those classes of types of activities which we have characterized as *compensatory* planning and *structural* planning (both individual and governmental) are invalid forms of planning. They are invalid because their empirical correlates in the natural order would violate the conditions of an effective plan. The remaining five classes of types of activities can all be valid (provided, of course, that other conditions of validity have been met, and then only within limits that are presently to be noted). These five classes are as follows:

1) $V''_k \cdot V'_k$,   stability planning
2) $V''_k \cdot V'_{i>k}$ individual developmental planning
3) $V''_{j>k} \cdot V'_k$,   governmental developmental planning
4) $V''_{j<k} \cdot V'_k$,   individual allocative planning
5) $V''_k \cdot V'_{i<k}$ governmental allocative planning

In all of these five classes of types of activities it is the case that either or both i, $j = k$. These activities can all be valid because their empirical correlates in the natural order comport with the conditions of an effective plan.

Yet the elements which will characterize every plan whose present normative content corresponds to the future empirical content of a natural order have not been fully identified. Still un-defined are some upper and lower limits beyond which no one sanction from a pair of sanctions can vary in respect to extremity —more precisely, how much variation in one value magnitude of a subset of activities can be valid when the other value magnitude has been fixed at k. Surely the fact that one component of a pair of sanctions is a motivating one gives us no warrant for supposing that the other component can take on any and every degree of over- or undermotivating extremity.

The limits to such variation are not hard to find. They reside in the two sets of boundary conditions which we established in Chapter IV for the state and the market. Those conditions set V''_{k-p} as the smallest subset of the state whose overlap with the market, in respect to value, is made up of activities that comport with an effective market; they set V'_{k-p} as the smallest subset of the market whose overlap with the state, in respect to value, is made up of activities that comport with an effective state. They further set V''_{k+q} as the largest subset of the state whose overlap with the market, in respect to value, is made up of activities that comport with an effective market; they set V'_{k+q} as the largest subset of the market whose overlap with the state, in respect to value, is made up of activities that comport with an effective state. Together these boundary conditions fix the limits of obedience and the limits of rationality. They thus formulate the minimum conditions for the coexistence of the state and the market as effective normative orders. Thereby too they formulate the minimum conditions for the efficacy of a plan. Any law which were to pre-scribe a sanction whose extremity exceeded V''_{k+q} or fell short of V''_{k-p} would violate the conditions of efficacy of the market; likewise any price which were to permit a sanction whose extremity exceeded V'_{k+q} or fell short of V'_{k-p} would violate the conditions of efficacy of the state. Hence any plan norm which were to include a law that prescribed a sanction more extreme than V''_{k+q} or less extreme than V''_{k-p} would be an invalid norm even if it also included a price that prescribed a sanction having the extremity V'_k. The same would be true of any plan norm which were to include a price having an excessive or deficient extremity in its sanction. It follows that the activities prescribed or permitted by such plan norms would be invalid, for they would be incompatible with the simultaneous efficacy of the state and the market as normative orders.

The limits, then, to the tolerable variation, with respect to extremity, which any one sanction out of a pair of sanctions can exhibit, are set by the following four types of activities: $V''_{k+q} \cdot V'_k$, $V''_k \cdot V'_{k+q}$, $V''_{k-p} \cdot V'_k$, and $V''_k \cdot V'_{k-p}$. These limits, located at four poles of the two chains which cross at $V''_k \cdot V'_k$, are surrogates, in the normative order, of some fundamental conditions of the natural order that a plan must meet if it is to be effective. They represent the maximum degrees of asymmetry, in respect to value, that can obtain in any set of activities which have been jointly prescribed by the state and permitted by the market. Perfect symmetry, to be sure, obtains in all of the stability types of activities. But radiating away from any such stability type of activity, such as $V''_k \cdot V'_k$, along the two chains which cross it in our lattice diagram, there is an increasing asymmetry as one approaches the limits that are represented by the four poles of the two chains.

In these limits to the asymmetry which may exist between the laws and the prices that jointly prescribe and permit a given type of activity we can claim to have finally identified just which types of activities may and may not be realized in the natural order of human behavior. Specifically it is the following types of activities, and these only, that may enter into a valid plan:

$$V''_k \cdot V'_i, \quad \text{and} \quad V''_j \cdot V'_k,$$

where $(k + q) \geqslant i, j \geqslant (k - p)$. Only these types of activities comport with the coexistence of both the state and the market and therefore with the existence of a plan as an effective normative order. In Figure 3 these types of activities all fall on the two heavy lines or chains which cross at the element $V''_k \cdot V'_k$. It is on these two chains, then, that we must expect to find the elements of every valid plan. It is these two chains which alone give a plan its structure and from which alone it derives its unity.

The vantage point now attained could not have been reached without the postulate of the mediate norm. It was this postulate which in the first place allowed coordination of the empirical events of the natural order with the prescribed and permitted events of a plan as a normative order, and which thereby allowed the determination of the limits of obedience and the limits of rationality in an effective plan. It was the mediate norm too which allowed the imposition of conceptual unity upon a collection of norms having two very different sources of validity, that is, laws (which owe their validity to the basic legal norm) and prices (which owe their validity to the basic economic norm); by relating these two different types of norms to a common condition of validity, namely, value, the mediate norm has become the means of revealing unity in any plan whose laws and prices answer to its stipulations.

From the vantage point thus attained it is possible to judge the validity or the invalidity of the norms of any historically given plan. From it too we can come to an appreciation of the considerable, though limited, variety of plans which may possess validity. Stability planning, developmental planning, and allocative planning are all valid types of planning, and they have all had their counterparts in history. Jurisprudential and economic doctrines which would deny validity to such plans can have little place in either the science or the art of planning. Finally, by means of the mediate norm we are compelled to recognize both the discrete individual and the collectivity as agents of effective planning. There are individual developmental plans and there are governmental developmental plans; there are individual allocative plans and there are governmental allocative plans; and all of them answer to the stipulations of the mediate norm. Effective planning, then, is planning which manages to combine the administrative decrees of a government with the incentives of individuals in a manner that reconciles obedience toward the one and rationality toward the other.

Yet in thus recognizing the dual reference of an effective plan to both the individual and the collectivity we find ourselves confronted with some unfinished business. The right of any one individual to be rational, after all, is predicated on the fact of widespread obedience to the government on the part of other individuals. So too, the obligation of the collectivity to enforce obedience finds its warrant in the extended scope for rationality which it offers to at least some individuals. Obedience and rationality thus have a behavioral as well as a normative reference. It is this behavioral aspect of obedience and rationality that must now be considered if final identification of the conditions of efficacy (and therefore of validity) of a plan is to be achieved.

CHAPTER VI

Conformity to Plans

> *Our rights are others' duties, secured*
> *in our behalf and belonging to us as*
> *our assets.*
>
> Leon Petrazycki[1]

P LANNING, unless it makes some difference in the real world, has little point. Indeed no plan can be valid unless it does make a difference—for efficacy is the first requisite of validity. Yet experience amply confirms the observation of the Scottish bard that even the best-laid plans "gang aft a-gley." In this imperfect relationship between present plans and future reality— between the normative and the natural—we encounter again the problem with which this study began: the problem of free will and determinism. However, some means of dealing with that problem now appear.

For one thing it is clear that a plan, viewed as a normative order, can *cause* nothing in the natural order. No relationship of causality exists between the "ought" or the "right," on the one hand, and the "is," on the other hand; the two realms represent entirely different epistemological constructions. Yet it is possible to assert that the content of a plan does or does not *correspond* with the content of future events. Indeed such a correspondence

---

[1] Leon Petrazycki, *Law and Morality,* trans. by Hugh W. Babb (Cambridge, Massachusetts: Harvard University Press, 1955), p. 46.

between the "ought" or the "right," on the one hand, and the "is," on the other hand, is a necessary condition for the validity of a plan's norms.

Conformity as a Correspondence between Plan and Reality

Manifestly, then, a pure theory of planning cannot ignore the nature of this correspondence between the normative and the natural. Its second task, after first establishing the conceptual categories that are presupposed in all knowledge about planning, must be to define the relationships between activities which are prescribed or permitted by the norms of a plan and the activities which are evident in the behavior of human beings. This task turns out to be an analysis of conformity and nonconformity, these being understood as particular relationships between the normative and the behavioral realms of events. Such an analysis is the subject of this chapter.

To ensure the consistency of the ensuing argument with what has preceded, its connection with the fundamental postulates which have guided the study must be established. These postulates are, of course, Kelsen's basic legal norm and the cognate basic economic norm. Both of these postulates, it will be recalled, find their justification in the fact that they allow the construction of two normative orders whose stipulated activities, in respect to content, correspond more closely to the events of the natural order than would the stipulated activities of any alternative order that might be derived from alternative postulates. In other words, the two basic norms are valid because the normative orders which they yield do for the most part correspond to the natural order. Thus the phenomenon of conformity has been implicit in our very choice of the basic legal norm and the basic economic norm.

Let us now consider this question: what would be the counterpart, in human behavior, of a normative order that was completely effective, such that every one of its stipulated activities was to find its realization in a corresponding event of the natural order? The basic legal norm could then be given the following behavioral translation: If the command of a supreme authority is violated, then coercive sanctions *will* be applied by that authority. Similarly the basic economic norm could be rendered as follows: If means are offered to an individual which are not those he is asking for, then that individual *will* either accept or reject the offer with a view to organizing his own complement of means into activities which will maximize his utility (want-gratification). The then-clauses of the contrapositives of these two behavioral postulates would be: (1) individuals *do* obey the commands of a supreme authority, and (2) individuals *do* offer one another means that they are asking for. More briefly:

1) Individuals are obedient, and
2) Individuals are rational.[2]

Each of these contrapositive then-clauses is a proposition concerning the behavior of individuals who confront the prospect of sanctions if they should behave otherwise. In other words individuals are obedient, in our hypothesized situation of a completely effective order, because, if they were not, coercive sanctions would be brought to bear upon them by a supreme authority. Likewise individuals are rational because, if they were not, their fellows would either accept or reject their offers by organizing their own complements of means into activities that would maximize their own utility (want-gratification) to the disadvantage of the offerers. Obedience and rationality, then, considered strictly as naturalistic phenomena, are behavioral corollaries of the sanctions that are described in the then-clauses of the behavioral translations of our two basic norms. In short, obedience and rationality are behavioral manifestations of conformity. All this, we must emphasize, applies only to the hypothetical case of a completely

[2] That is, at general equilibrium it is rational for every participant in the Walrasian market to eventually equate his offers of means to the demands of others.

effective normative order whose every prescription and every permission were to find its realization in empirical reality.

Characteristics of Conforming and Nonconforming Behavior

A normative order of this kind, of course, can have only an epiphenomenal status; it can be no more than a passive reflex of the natural order, predicting the latter's properties but having no epistemological independence of its own. Yet as a hypothetical construction it should help us to an understanding of two fundamental features of conforming and nonconforming behavior: (1) the complementary relationship which obtains between obedience on the part of one individual and rationality on the part of another individual; and (2) the variable psychological balance between want-gratification and want-deprivation which attends different types of activities viewed in terms of the degree of obedience and rationality that they require of an individual. A brief consideration of these two features of conforming behavior, within the frame of reference of the hypothetical case of a completely effective normative order, should provide a firm vantage point from which to then undertake a lengthier analysis of conformity and nonconformity as it obtains in the different types of activities that characterize an effective plan.

THE COMPLEMENTARITY OF OBEDIENCE AND RATIONALITY

We have had previous occasion to note that in every overlap between the market and the state there is a complementarity between the right of an individual to be rational and the obligation of other individuals to obey a supreme authority. That is to say, the right of an individual to be rational is predicated on the obligation of other individuals not to obstruct him in his rationality—that is, an obligation on their part to obey the laws of the state. So too the obligation of an individual to obey the supreme authority presupposes the right of other individuals to be rational; that, indeed, is the whole *raison d'être* of obedience. This complemen-

tarity of rights and obligations is characteristic of every intersection $V''_i \cdot V'_j$ between a subset of activities prescribed by the
state and a subset of activities permitted by the market. Assuming, now, that a completely effective normative order exists, it is
evident that the same complementarity should obtain between
rationality, considered as a behavioral datum, and obedience, considered as a behavioral datum. We should expect to find a complementarity between obedience and rationality in every subset
(x''_i, x'_j) of empirical activities in the natural order. Each such
subset, in other words, can be regarded as a collection of activities
to which attaches a certain degree of obedience and a certain degree of rationality, these being considered now as strictly behavioral phenomena. The degree of such obedience and the degree
of such rationality will correspond to the extremities of the sanctions which have been specified in the then-clauses of the laws
and the prices that prescribe and permit the activities comprising
the given subset.

The essential form of this complementary relationship between
the obedience of one individual and the rationality of others can
be seen in the phenomenon of the contract. A contract belongs to
both the state and the market. The terms of a contract, though
freely arrived at by rational individuals who are seeking to maximize their want-gratification in the market, remain legally obligatory for all of them, even if unforeseen circumstances should
happen to render those terms disadvantageous to some of the individuals. The full force of the state stands behind the terms of a
contract. Hence the rationality which initially expressed itself in
the terms of a contract finds its complement in the assured obedience of every signatory, even when the bargain proves to have
been a bad one for some of them. Obedience, in its turn, finds its
raison d'être in the support which it gives to the subsequent exercise of rationality. Without assured obedience to the terms of a
contract there could literally be no rationality, for agreed-upon
contractual terms could then have no more than a moment-by-

moment efficacy, vitiating the whole point to rational calculation of future advantage.

THE VARIABLE RATIO BETWEEN WANT-GRATIFICATION AND WANT-DEPRIVATION

In our preceding chapter we took note of the strain which is imposed on human beings by activities whose nonperformance entails overmotivating or undermotivating sanctions. Conformity to such activities imposes want-deprivations on individuals which in turn give rise to very real psychological tensions. The locus of these tensions is intraindividual but their genesis is interindividual.[3] In a completely effective normative order, to be sure, these tensions would have no effect upon behavior. Individuals would be obedient and they would be rational, in due proportion to the extremities of the sanctions which were provided by the relevant laws and prices. Yet the psychological tensions would still be there. What is their essential form? The answer to this question will help predict the consequences of over- and undermotivating sanctions in plans that are less than completely effective. Such plans, after all, are the only ones vouchsafed to us by observation, and they are the ones which will be presently considered.

The fundamental fact about want-gratification and want-deprivation is its interindividual character. To be sure, it is the discrete individual who, in the market, seeks to maximize his want-gratification up to the limit of the means available to him; and it is the discrete individual who, in the state, tends to acquiesce in want-deprivation to the extent required by the coercive power of government. Even more, it is the discrete individual who, in the process of acquiring what might be called "character," has learned that he feels better when he voluntarily

[3] Talcott Parsons, *The Social System* (New York: The Free Press of Glencoe, Inc., 1951), Chapters VI–VII.

tempers his want-gratification with some measure of want-deprivation. But this very impulse toward the "optimization of gratification"[4] has its origins outside the self. It has its origins in the give-and-take among interdependent individuals whose need for one another, overriding their interest in maximum want-gratification, expresses itself in a willing acceptance of some degree of want-deprivation. Moreover, the measure of optimization itself has its origins outside the self. It resides in the comparisons which individuals are constantly making of the various degrees of want-gratification and want-deprivation which inevitably obtain among themselves. Any activity, therefore, whose nonperformance entails two sanctions of differing extremities—one of them in the state, and the other in the market—will give rise to a sense of relative disadvantage on the part of those particular individuals who, in a given situation, are faced with the more extreme sanction while other individuals, in that same situation, confront the less extreme sanction. That is, the incidence of any two sanctions upon a population of individuals will never be uniform, owing to the differing situations which those individuals invariably occupy on any one occasion, the result being that some individuals are going to confront an obedience-disobedience choice, and others are going to confront a rationality-irrationality choice. Tolerance for some portion of these inequities is a ubiquitous feature of the civilized human personality. An effective normative order, then, is one whose human agents have learned to spontaneously seek a prudent balance between want-gratification and want-deprivation, freely participating in activities that vary widely in respect to that dimension, and preferring the security of such a balance to the insecurity of any excess.

Such conformity, however, is fraught with its own costs: obedience is hard on the self; rationality is hard on others (and,

[4] *Ibid.*, p. 5.

likewise, on the self to whom those others matter). In the first instance ". . . obedience to duty means resistance to self,"[5] resistance to πλεονεξία, resistance to ". . . immediate perception of self-interest, . . ."[6] with all the tensions that inhere in such want-deprivations. In the second case, the rationality of an individual can upset others' expectations, violate confidences, and weaken that *Rechtsgefühl* which is the mark of every civilized person, again carrying with it a whole train of psychological tensions— among them a bad conscience. These consequences of obedience and rationality are inherent in every natural order of human behavior, though in our hypothetical case of a completely effective order they would only be latent rather than manifest.

It is when attention turns from the hypothetical to the real, however, that this perspective on conforming behavior, focused as it has been on the complementary nature of obedience and rationality and on the variable character of the ratio between want-gratification and want-deprivation, turns out to be productive of insight into the nature and consequences of conformity in different types of activities. Let us bring our perspective to bear, then, on the analysis of a normative order which is imperfectly effective, in the sense that while most of its activities do get realized in the natural order, some of them do not. Every such order will be one that includes among its stipulated activities some which are not fully observed by its human agents. So long as those activities are not too numerous they will of course retain their validity. Yet the fact remains that the order to which they belong is being imperfectly realized in the behavior of its human agents. What is the scope and what is the significance of such noncon-

[5] Henri Bergson, *The Two Sources of Morality and Religion*, trans. by A. Ashley Audra and Cloudesely Brereton (New York: Holt, Rinehart and Winston, Inc., 1935, 1963), p. 12.

[6] Max Rheinstein (ed.), *Max Weber on Law in Economy and Society*, trans. by Max Rheinstein and Edward A. Shils (Cambridge, Massachusetts: Harvard University Press, 1954), p. 37.

formity in the different types of planning that have been identified in Chapter V?

THE BEHAVIORAL SIGNIFICANCE OF SANCTIONS

To begin with, obedience and rationality are matters of degree, varying with respect to the sanctions which motivate them and with respect to the consequences which follow from them for the efficacy of a normative order. This fact can be inferred from the behavioral rendition of the mediate norm which was advanced in the preceding chapter and from the comparable rendition of the two basic norms which has just been advanced in this chapter.

The first of our behavioral translations—this one of the mediate norm—allows us to conceive of sanctions as varying over overmotivating, motivating, and undermotivating extremities, these being considered now as naturalistic, psychological magnitudes. All of these different extremities of sanctions, of course, will have been specified in the then-clauses of various laws and prices as conditionally consequent upon specified acts of disobedience or irrationality. The same behavioral translation of the mediate norm allows us to assert a relationship between different extremities of sanctions, on the one hand, and the corresponding magnitudes of contribution which various activities (to whose nonperformance the sanctions attach) make to the efficacy of their order.

The second of our behavioral translations, applied to the two basic norms, allows us to express obedience and rationality—again considered as naturalistic phenomena—as logical consequents of the nonimposition of available sanctions. This relationship finds its formulation in the two contrapositives of the behavioral renditions of the two basic norms:

1) If coercive sanctions are not applied by a supreme authority, then the commands of that authority have been obeyed; and

2) If an individual does not react to an offer of means by organizing his own complement of means so as to increase his utility, then the offered means were those he had been asking for.

Insofar, now, as a normative order is an effective one—albeit imperfectly so—these propositions become descriptive of actual behavior: sanctions will not generally be applied, and individuals will generally be both obedient and rational. The sanctions, of course, do have to be available for the occasional lapse; by hypothesis, after all, they constitute necessary conditions for the efficacy of the order to which they belong.

We now put our two behavioral translations together and come up with the following conclusions:

1) Overmotivating laws and prices are sufficient conditions for strict obedience and strict rationality, respectively.

1') Strict obedience and strict rationality stand in correspondence with a high contribution on the part of the relevant activities to the efficacy of their order(that is, they stand in correspondence with a high degree of dependency, relative to the attribute of want-gratification, between any such activity and the remaining activities in its order).

2) Motivating laws and prices are sufficient conditions for obedience and rationality, respectively.

2') Obedience and rationality stand in correspondence with an intermediate contribution on the part of the relevant activities to the efficacy of their order (that is, they stand in correspondence with an intermediate degree of dependency, relative to the attribute of want-gratification, between any such activity and the remaining activities in its order).

3) Undermotivating laws and prices are sufficient conditions for indifferent obedience and indifferent rationality, respectively.

3') Indifferent obedience and indifferent rationality stand in correspondence with a low contribution on the part of the relevant activities to the efficacy of their order (that is, they stand in correspondence with a low degree of dependency, relative to the attribute of want-gratification, between any such activity and the remaining activities in its order).

These are important conclusions. They allow the interpretation of obedience and rationality as matters of degree, and they allow the relating of such degrees of conforming behavior, on the one hand, to the sanctions that characterize a natural order of human behavior and, on the other hand, to the contribution which the relevant activities make to the efficacy of their order. In so doing they prepare the way for the next step in the argument, which will consist of relating conformity and nonconformity to the various classes of planning that were identified in the preceding chapter.

In establishing these relationships, however, a precise explication of "degrees" of obedience and "degrees" of rationality is needed. Obedience and rationality, we have noted, are the behavioral manifestations of conformity. As such they vary over a wide range from strict obedience and strict rationality to indifferent obedience and indifferent rationality. Strictness and indifference, for their part, are simply ratios between the number of occasions in which a prescribed or permitted activity is performed and the number of occasions in which that activity is supposed to be performed. A high ratio indicates a close correspondence between the behavioral and the normative realms of events—namely, conformity, as manifest in strict obedience or strict rationality. A low ratio indicates a poor correspondence

between the behavioral and the normative realms of events—
namely, nonconformity, as manifest in indifferent obedience or
indifferent rationality.

Obedience and Rationality in Different Types of Plans

A new question now arises: how much obedience and how much
rationality are required by the various kinds of valid plan activities which have been identified in the preceding chapter?
Along with this question arises another one: what are the consequences for want-gratification and want-deprivation of the various
degrees of obedience and rationality that are called for by different types of plan activities?[7] A plan, we should remind ourselves, is a normative order which endows certain designated
agents with the obligation or the right to impose sanctions on any
other agent who fails to perform some specified activities. In an
effective plan there is a correspondence between the present
content of these prescribed and permitted activities and the future
content of actual activities in the natural order. To the subset
$V''_i.V'_j$ of activities in a plan there corresponds a subset (x''_i, x'_j)
of empirical activities. The contribution which these activities
make to the efficacy of their total order may be high or it may be
low. If the contribution is high we should expect the activities to
entail strict obedience or strict rationality, along with overmotivating laws or overmotivating prices. If the contribution is low we
should expect the activities to entail indifferent obedience or indifferent rationality, along with undermotivating laws or undermotivating prices. In the former case we should look for one
pattern of psychological tensions, in the latter case for another
pattern of tensions, each, however, manifesting a faulty balance
between want-gratification and want-deprivation.

[7] The solutions presented in reference to these two questions rest on
Sorokin's analysis of concordant and discordant norms. See Pitirim A.
Sorokin, *Society, Culture, and Personality* (New York: Harper and Row,
1947), pp. 121–128.

In the preceding chapter we identified five distinct classes of such plan activities. Translated into their behavioral versions they are as follows:

1) (x''_k, x'_k), constituting stability plans

2) $(x''_k, x'_{i>k})$, constituting individual developmental plans

3) $(x''_{j>k}, x'_k)$, constituting governmental developmental plans

4) $(x''_{j<k}, x'_k)$, constituting individual allocative plans

5) $(x''_k, x'_{i<k})$, constituting governmental allocative plans

Let us now consider each of these classes of activities, along with the plans which comprise them, with a view to better understanding the significance of conformity and nonconformity in various forms of social and economic planning. In doing so we should keep in mind the obvious fact that our five classes of valid plan activities are no more than typological constructions; any historically given plan, therefore, will consist of activities from any or all of these five classes.

To facilitate the analysis only one kind of planning—that of capital formation—will be investigated. The generalized import of the analysis, however, should be apparent throughout. Capital, after all, derives its significance from the contribution which its associated activities make to the efficacy of a normative order. Specifically, over a very broad range of variation in intensity, capital increases the degree of dependency which holds, with respect to the attribute of want-gratification, between a given activity and the remaining activities of its order. It is this feature which gives this analysis its generalized significance for a theory of planning. The term *capital formation* will include the whole spectrum of investment processes ranging from capital accumulation to capital depreciation, the former being associated with a high contribution, the latter with a low contribution, to the efficacy of a normative order. In an analysis with strictly typological purposes, as the following, it has not seemed appropriate to observe theoretical refinements that would be essential in a thoroughgoing treatment of capital theory.

One necessary condition for capital accumulation, of course, is a high saving-income ratio; a necessary condition for capital depreciation is a low saving-income ratio. But saving can only lead to capital formation if it is accompanied by investment through the mechanisms of lending and borrowing. Lending and borrowing, in their turn, presuppose either rationality (if they are voluntary) or obedience (if they are involuntary). In either case lending and borrowing represent behavior contrary to that which would entail the sanctions that are specified in the then-clause of a price or the then-clause of a law. The extent of lending and borrowing will be proportional to the extremities of those sanctions; hence high saving and investment rates will be associated with overmotivating sanctions, and low saving and investment rates will be associated with undermotivating sanctions. The consequences of saving and investment behavior, in turn, may run the whole gamut of want-gratification and want-deprivation.

STABILITY PLANS

Stability plans occupy an intermediate position on all of these variables. Stability plans, it should be remarked, can have a multitude of discrete individuals as their agents, or they may have the government as their agent. In the former case they approximate, more than any other class of activities, the voluntary, decentralized market that was formalized by Walras; in the latter case they represent a governmental simulation of such a market. The essential feature of stability plans lies in the symmetrical relationship which obtains between the extremity of sanctions that are specified by laws and the extremity of sanctions that are specified by prices, combined with the equal incidence which these contingent sanctions have upon every agent. In such a market for capital goods, lenders and borrowers, as discrete individuals, enter freely into exchange relationships the terms of which are governed, on the one hand, by the law of contract and, on the other hand, by the price of capital (the interest rate).

In the first instance lenders and borrowers are motivated to obey legal proscriptions against usury, fraud, hoarding, servitude, nonrepayment, etc.; they are motivated to pay whatever taxes the government may have levied and to buy whatever bonds it may have issued with a view to increasing the rate of saving; and they are motivated to expand or curtail their saving by legally specified down-payment requirements. Some observance of these norms characterizes all stability activities in which there is lending and borrowing. The sanctions which are contingent upon their possible nonobservance consist of fine, imprisonment, loss of credit, etc.

In the second instance lenders and borrowers are motivated to maximize want-gratification over time up to the limit of their present and future means. This is possible only when, for lender and borrower alike, the marginal rate of substitution between means available for present ends and means available for future ends is equal to the ratio of the prices of those respective means (including interest). For its part the rate of interest tends to a level that will equate saving and the demand for capital, this of course being one of the requirements of a general market equilibrium. The sanctions which are contingent upon the possible nonobservance of these conditions consist of restrictions on the range of alternative means that would otherwise have been available to a lender or borrower, such restrictions taking the form of an oversupply or undersupply of capital.

What, now, is the extremity of the sanctions—both legal and economic—which will characterize lending and borrowing in stability plans? In our previous chapter we were led to conclude that at least one component of the pair of sanctions which attaches to every activity of a valid plan must be a motivating sanction rather than an over- or undermotivating sanction. Since, then, the activities which comprise a stability plan are characterized by equality as between the sanctions prescribed by laws and the sanctions permitted by prices, it follows that *both* components of every pair of sanctions in stability plans will be motivating sanctions. Hence all of the activities of an effective stability plan fall within the subset (x''_k, x'_k).

It follows that lending and borrowing in stability plans constitutes motivated, but not over- or undermotivated behavior. As such it involves an intermediate degree of obedience and an intermediate degree of rationality, these being the behavioral corollaries of motivating sanctions. Instances of disobedience do of course occur: when savers lend at usurious rates or take advantage of borrowers' ignorance; or when borrowers renege on repayment or indulge in tax-evasion schemes. So too there are instances of irrationality in which savers lend to poor credit risks or extend interest-free loans to friends and relatives—instances too in which borrowers fail to obtain the best possible credit terms or overextend their indebtedness. Such nonconforming behavior, however, is sufficiently infrequent that it entails little impairment of the efficacy of a stability plan.

The intermediate degree of obedience and rationality which characterizes a stability plan comports with a gratification-deprivation balance that is more or less predictable and expected by its human agents. In particular there is equality among the agents of a stability plan in respect to want-gratification and want-deprivation. This equality is ensured by the fact that rationality induces different agents to lend and borrow until their respective marginal rates of time substitution between present means and future means are equal, at which point there is equal gratification of the relevant wants among those agents. It is further ensured by the equal incidence which legal and economic sanctions have upon every agent in a stability plan. Such interpersonal equality in want-gratification and want-deprivation minimizes the strain which is imposed on human beings by activities which involve lending and borrowing.

What, now, will be the rate of capital formation that is afforded by stability planning? This too turns out to be an intermediate magnitude. The rate of capital formation in a stability plan will vary with the interest rate, that being the price which equates the supply of capital with the demand for capital. Hence capital formation in a stability plan is subject to all the stimulation and all the inhibition which inheres in the pricing process of a voluntary, decentralized market. Under these conditions the rate of capital formation will be just exactly that which "pays"—no more and no less. This rate will perforce correspond with the rate which is implied by the laws of the state.

DEVELOPMENTAL AND ALLOCATIVE PLANS

Developmental and allocative plans, both individual and governmental, present a rather different picture. The essential feature of developmental and allocative plans lies in the asymmetrical relationship which obtains between legal and economic sanctions, one of them being over- or undermotivating, the other being motivating, the two of them having unequal incidence upon different agents. This asymmetry in the sanctions of a developmental or allocative plan affects the rate of capital formation through its influence on the lending and borrowing behavior of individuals.

In individual developmental plans the sanctions of the market are overmotivating and those of the state are motivating; in governmental developmental plans the sanctions of the state are overmotivating and those of the market are motivating. So too, in individual allocative plans the sanctions of the market are motivating and those of the state are undermotivating; in governmental allocative plans the sanctions of the state are motivating and those of the market are undermotivating. Correspondingly one finds individual developmental plans characterized by strict rationality and intermediate obedience; governmental developmental plans are characterized by strict obedience and intermediate rationality. Individual allocative plans, on the other hand, are characterized by intermediate rationality and indifferent obedience; governmental allocative plans are characterized by intermediate obedience and indifferent rationality. These characteristics, summarized in the accompanying table, are simply the behavioral versions of Classes 2–5 of the types of valid activities set forth in Chapter V. The pertinent features of capital formation that are associated with these different types of planning are considered below.

INDIVIDUAL DEVELOPMENTAL PLANS

In individual developmental plans capital formation may have its "origin" in either investment demand or saving (though ultimately both are prerequisite to it). In the first case the investor is an individual whose ingenuity has been challenged by the development of new technical processes, new natural resources, improved administrative procedures, or some other important innovation. Under his aegis these developments become investment opportunities which, by increasing the demand for capital, raise interest rates and confront prospective lenders with a chance for greater profits. The possibility of forfeiting such profits becomes an overmotivating sanction which induces lenders to increase their rate of saving beyond the level which a general market equilibrium would warrant. Such behavior on the part of lenders is strictly rational.

On the saving side, capital formation in individual developmental plans may originate in a widespread attitude of worldly asceticism combined with a disciplined acquisitiveness (Weber's "spirit of capitalism"). Individuals who are thus motivated will have high saving-income ratios. The resulting volume of saving leads to low interest rates and to an opportunity for investors to

Developmental and Allocative Plans
Summary of Characteristics

Types of Planning	Extremity of Sanctions		Degree of Conforming Behavior	
	Laws	Prices	Obedience	Rationality
Developmental:				
Individual	Motivating	Over-motivating	Intermediate	Strict
Governmental	Over-motivating	Motivating	Strict	Intermediate
Allocative:				
Individual	Under-motivating	Motivating	Indifferent	Intermediate
Governmental	Motivating	Under-motivating	Intermediate	Indifferent

borrow and invest advantageously. The possibility of forfeiting high rates of profit becomes an overmotivating sanction which induces borrowers to increase their rate of investment beyond the level which a general market equilibrium would warrant. Such behavior on the part of borrowers is strictly rational.

Thus, whether its "origin" lies on the demand side or on the supply side, capital formation in individual developmental plans is a response to overmotivating sanctions in the market. To a much lesser degree it is a response to the motivating sanctions of the state. In other words, capital formation in individual developmental plans has its origin primarily in the market rather than in the state. Hence, in contrast to the symmetry which obtains between the prices and the laws of a stability plan, there is an asymmetry between the prices and the laws of individual developmental plans. This asymmetry means that the sanctions of the market bear more heavily upon the *irrational* lender or borrower than do the sanctions of the state upon the *disobedient* lender or borrower. It means that the state, with its motivating (rather than overmotivating) sanctions, does not fully support the activities of an individual developmental plan. Hence the individual in a lending-borrowing relationship whose opposite number has failed to observe the terms of a contract—for example, a mortgage loan or a commercial loan—will get less support from the state than he will from the market in bringing sanctions to bear on the offender. The government, for example, may guarantee certain mortgage loans, but only up to a stipulated amount; beyond that the unfortunate lender will not be able to enlist the support of the state on his behalf. So too the borrower who becomes insolvent through circumstances beyond his control can declare himself bankrupt; beyond that, however, the unfortunate borrower will get no support from the state against economic reprisals which the lender may inflict upon him.

An important corollary of this asymmetry lies in the unequal incidence which legal and economic sanctions have upon the various agents of an individual developmental plan. Thus an individual whose nonobservance of an activity in an individual developmental plan consists of a disadvantageous but legal loan would confront more extreme sanctions in the market than an individual whose nonobservance of the same activity consists of a violation of the law of contract would confront in the state. Avoidance of these respective sanctions, taking the form of strict rationality on the part of the first individual and obedience on the part of the second individual, results in an inequality among those agents with respect to want-gratification and want-deprivation. This inequality manifests itself in differing rather than equal marginal rates of time substitution between present means and future means as between various agents, quite in contrast to the situation which characterizes stability planning. It manifests itself too in the unequal honoring of interpersonal expectations and confidences on the part of the strictly rational individual versus the obedient individual. Such inequalities among the agents of an individual developmental plan, with respect to want-gratification and want-deprivation, generate psychological tensions which react upon the plan in ways presently to be considered.

Despite these tensions, though, individual developmental planning is capable of yielding high rates of capital formation. It is inefficient, by marginalist criteria, but it is effective. Indeed, in terms of future want-gratification, its yield in increased productivity can more than outweigh its allocative inefficiency. Moreover, by its apportioning of capital among different sectors of the economy it can be an instrument for determining, not only the rate of development, but also the direction of development.

GOVERNMENTAL DEVELOPMENTAL PLANS

The same is true of capital formation in governmental developmental plans, though the *modus operandi* here is somewhat different. The government, as an agent of the collectivity, is in a position to resolve differing opinions concerning desirable rates and directions of economic growth. Moreover, as the agent which is possessed of maximum power, it is in a position to implement its decisions on behalf of the collectivity. In governmental developmental planning capital formation has its proximate "origin" in investment demand, as determined by the government, and in saving, again as determined by the government. Both of these quantities are matters for political decision. In an ultimate sense, to be sure, investment and saving rates are limited, as in every type of planning, by basic dependency relations inherent in the natural order of human behavior. The political decisions, therefore, which enter into a governmental developmental plan will be effective to the degree that they reckon with such dependency relations.

Within broad limits, then, a government can fix investment and saving rates either directly, or by manipulating interest rates and other prices. As a borrower the government can raise capital funds by tax levies, the sale of bonds, expropriation, etc. The funds so raised can then be allocated to various enterprises through grants and loans, the terms of such relationships again being determined by the government.

Capital formation in governmental developmental plans is a response to overmotivating sanctions in the state. To a lesser degree it is a response to the motivating sanctions of the market. An asymmetry exists, then, as with individual developmental plans, between the laws and the prices of governmental developmental plans. In the present case, however, it is the disobedient individual, rather than the irrational individual, who incurs the more extreme sanctions. Strict obedience, it appears, is the *sine qua non* of governmental developmental plans; payment of taxes, the purchase of bonds, even at times the compulsory delivery of produce, may all be essential for their capital formation. Individual rationality, on the other hand, is less supportive of governmental developmental plans; lending, for example, may take place on terms that are quite disadvantageous to the individual (though the eventual outcome can be a general market equilibrium which is on a much higher level than the one attainable through a stability plan).

Want-gratification and want-deprivation under a governmental developmental plan may sometimes approach equality among individuals, depending on the objectives of the plan. However, some imbalance in want-gratification and want-deprivation is invariably created by the strict obedience and the moderate rationality which such a plan involves. Through various mechanisms of reality-testing individuals almost inevitably develop an awareness of the relative disadvantage which they incur, in respect to want-gratification, by conforming to the activities of a governmental developmental plan. The existence of a private sector in the economy, for example, or the presence of a black market, or an influx of information from other societies, combined with any inequality in respect to want-gratification which may exist within a population, all provide individuals with a measure of the relative disadvantage which is entailed by their strict obedience to the norms of such a plan. This relative disadvantage precludes an "optimization of gratification" and it generates tensions which react upon the plan itself. The nature of this reaction will be discussed toward the close of the chapter.

It is probable that historically the very highest rates of capital formation have been those which were attained under governmental developmental plans. It is probable too that the most consistently directional capital formation, in terms of the maintenance of stable priorities among different sectors of the economy, has again been that of governmental developmental plans. In such plans the rates and directions of growth are political decisions, and their constancy or variation over time is to be explained in terms of political variables. While this is no way gainsays the dependence of such variables upon other variables, it does quite properly emphasize the element of volition in economic planning. It also reminds us that political developments can affect the course and outcome of capital formation in any society.

INDIVIDUAL ALLOCATIVE PLANS

Individual allocative plans differ from individual developmental plans in respect to the positions which their activities occupy on the various variables with which our analysis has been concerned. In particular, individual allocative plans involve low rates of capital formation (including at times even negative rates —that is, capital depreciation). Investment demand may be quite sufficient to generate the interest rates that would attract lenders, and saving rates may be high enough to create the volume of capital which is prerequisite to the interest rates that would attract borrowers. Nevertheless saving and investment rates are below those of developmental plans and they are even lower than those of stability plans. The reason for this lies in the nonsupportive role of the state vis-a-vis capital formation. Nonperformance of the activities of an individual allocative plan entails no more than undermotivating sanctions from the state; it entails motivating sanctions from the market. Tribute, booty, private monopoly of investment funds, and "combinations in restraint of trade" all find greater support in the market than they do in the state; their nonperformance entails more drastic sanctions from the market than they do from the state.

Irrationality, then, is penalized more than disobedience, in individual allocative plans; neither, however, is penalized as severely as they are in individual developmental plans. Hence rationality and indifferent obedience are characteristic of the agents of individual allocative plans. Furthermore, the unequal incidence which economic and legal sanctions have upon different agents, leading to rationality by one individual and indifferent obedience by another, results in an inequality among individuals with respect to want-gratification and want-deprivation. This in turn generates psychological tensions of the kind which characterize individual developmental plans, though the magnitude of these tensions is less in individual allocative plans.

With sanctions of relatively low extremity, and with conformity that is correspondingly low, it is not surprising that individual allocative plans are characterized by low rates of capital formation.

GOVERNMENTAL ALLOCATIVE PLANS

Our final class of plan activities consists of those which constitute governmental allocative plans. In such plans, saving and investment rates are determined by the government. In contrast to governmental developmental plans, however, saving and investment rates are low. Behind these low rates lie the motivating sanctions of the state and the undermotivating sanctions of the market. Disobedience is penalized more severely than irrationality; neither, however, is penalized as severely as in governmental developmental plans. The most, therefore, that can be expected in governmental allocative plans is obedience, on the one hand, and indifferent rationality on the other.

Defense projects, welfare programs, and the taxation of venture capital are representative of such plans. Nonperformance of any of their activities, through profiteering, sabotage, tax evasion and the like entails more drastic sanctions from the state than it does from the market.

There is, in governmental allocative plans, the same kind of imbalance, with respect to want-gratification and want-deprivation, that there is in governmental developmental plans. However, the degree of disadvantage which individuals experience through obeying the norms of a governmental allocative plan is less than it is in governmental developmental plans. The tensions which result from such disadvantage are accordingly weaker, though they are sufficient to exert some reaction upon the plan.

Associated with all these features of governmental allocative plans we find low rates of capital formation.

It is only rarely, of course, that the activities of a historically given plan will fall neatly into only one of the five classes of valid plan activities. In nearly every real plan for capital formation the component activities will show a wide range of variation over the variables with which we have been concerned, with the result that they will occupy several or all of the five classes of planning. For this reason the overall rate of capital formation in any actual plan becomes an exceedingly complicated function.

From the foregoing analysis it should be clear that conformity is a rather variable quantity as between different kinds of plans, its magnitude or degree being a function of the extremity of the sanctions which apply to the activities that comprise those plans. It is clear too that the magnitude of want-gratification or want-deprivation is another variable quantity among different kinds of plans. Further, we have seen that the relative incidence which both of these quantities have upon different individuals can vary all the way from equality, in the case of stability plans, to inequality, in the case of developmental and allocative plans. Finally, we have noted that any inequality in the incidence of want-gratification and want-deprivation as between the various agents of a plan is associated with the emergence of psychological tensions among those individuals.

Anomalous Activities and the Resistance to Plans

There is now the task of examining the significance of these psychological tensions. Already there has been occasion to observe (in Chapter V) that overmotivating sanctions are associated, not only with strict conformity, but also with some anomalous activities: covert subversion, obsessive behavior, and passive withdrawal. Likewise undermotivating sanctions are associated, not only with indifferent conformity, but also with anomalous activities like duplicity, opportunism, and apathy. These anomalous activities, it may be suggested, are the overt manifestation of the psychological tensions which arise out of interpersonal inequalities in want-gratification and want-deprivation, these in turn being a result of the differential incidence which sanctions of unequal extremity have upon a population of interrelated individuals. Anomalous activities are therefore inherent in all developmental and allocative plans. They are not characteristic of stability plans.

Anomalous activities are the behavioral counterparts, in the natural realm, of some normatively prescribed or permitted activities. But unlike the activities of the state or the market the normative surrogates of anomalous activities are inconsistent with the basic legal norm and with the basic economic norm. Hence those surrogates have no validity, despite the empirical reality of their behavioral counterparts. Their significance lies in the resistance which they present to the inequitable demands placed by valid activities upon a population of interrelated but differently situated individuals. A special case of the phenomenon can be seen in the "countervailing power" so characteristic of modern American capitalism.[8] More generally: governmental plans (either developmental or allocative) typically give rise to such activities as black markets, tax evasion, profiteering, and sabotage; individual plans (either developmental or allocative) typically lead to featherbedding, subsidization, and protective legislation.

Whenever conformity to a subset of valid activities is unequally demanding of various individuals, thereby creating an interpersonal imbalance in gratification and deprivation, the disadvantaged individuals are going to have recourse to another subset of activities—anomalous activities—which have the effect of partially neutralizing the first subset of activities. Inequitable demands from the state will impel disadvantaged individuals to seek refuge in invalid "market" activities; inequitable demands from the market will drive disadvantaged individuals into invalid "state" activities. These invalid activities in turn become normalized as "adaptive structures,"[9] in which capacity they exert an inhibiting influence upon the valid activities to which they were a reaction.

The impulse to engage in such anomalous activities is in direct proportion to the degree of inequality which obtains among individuals with regard to want-gratification and want-deprivation. The sanctions which sustain a subset of anomalous activities have the same extremity as those which sustain the subset of valid activities to which those anomalous activities are a reaction. There is this difference, however: the extremity of legal sanctions becomes interchanged with that of economic sanctions, so that what was more motivating in a valid activity becomes less motivating in the corresponding anomalous activity, and vice versa.

[8] John Kenneth Galbraith, *American Capitalism,* second ed. (Boston: Houghton Mifflin Co., 1956).

[9] Parsons, *The Social System,* pp. 167–168.

These propositions may be given concise formulation in the following two universally quantified equivalences:

$$[(x''_j, x'_i) \leqslant Y] \equiv [(x''_i, x'_j) \leqslant X]$$
$$[(x''_i, x'_j) \leqslant Y] \equiv [(x''_j, x'_i) \leqslant X]$$

where $i < j$. In these equivalences the term (x''_i, x'_j) represents, as before, a subset of empirical activities, one of whose sanctions is specified by a law, the other of whose sanctions is specified by a price, these sanctions having the extremities of i and j, respectively; X represents the subset of activities which comprise a plan; (x''_j, x'_i) represents another subset of empirical activities whose legal and economic sanctions have the indicated extremities; and Y represents the subset of anomalous activities.

The first of these propositions states a necessary and sufficient condition for the inclusion of: (1) a subset of activities whose pair of sanctions have extremities of j and i in: (2) a subset of anomalous activities. This necessary and sufficient condition is the inclusion of: (1) a subset of activities whose pair of sanctions have extremities of i and j in: (2) a subset of plan activities. The second proposition states a similar relationship for the subsets of activities (x''_i, x'_j) and (x''_j, x'_i), respectively. Together the two propositions assert that a nonstability plan is a necessary and sufficient condition of anomalous activities.

In other words, a developmental or allocative plan which includes the subset (x''_i, x'_j) in its repertoire of activities, thereby demanding more rationality than obedience of its human subjects, will perforce generate a subset (x''_j, x'_i) of anomalous activities which involve more obedience than rationality. Such obedience, of course, will be directed to various private and extralegal authorities rather than to the government. Conversely a plan which includes (x''_j, x'_i) in its repertoire of activities, thus demanding more obedience than rationality, will generate a subset (x''_i, x'_j) of anomalous activities which involve more rationality than obedience. Such rationality, for its part, will manifest itself in various interstitial and *sub rosa* markets rather than in the general market.

The practical significance of this hypothesis lies in the fact that every developmental or allocative plan is invariably confronted with nonconforming responses which can at times subvert its objectives. These nonconforming responses are of a very different magnitude from the nonconformity which marks stability plans. Whereas the latter is random and *ad hoc,* the former is consistent and systematic. Where the former can be condoned or appeased, the latter must be suppressed or pre-empted. The one does no more than impose costs upon a plan; the other threatens the very efficacy of the plan itself.

Both kinds of nonconformity, however, account for the fundamental fact that human beings, as elements of the natural order, are somewhat refractory to the planning process. Plans "gang aft a-gley" because people do not conform to them. Yet there are plans which work. There are plans which make a difference in the real world. These plans owe all their success to the obedience and the rationality of their human agents.

CHAPTER VII

The Reality of Planning

*In a general way, reality is ordered
exactly to the degree in which it sat-
isfies our thought.*

Henri Bergson[1]

TWO KINDS of societies exist in popular thinking: the planned and the unplanned. One of them is considered good, the other, bad. Yet the argument set forth in this study would suggest that the distinction is really one without a difference. Every society has its plans; indeed, every society has *a* plan. The more pertinent distinction, then, would seem to be one between societies in which planning is the obligation of the government, and societies in which planning is the right of discrete individuals.

Yet even this distinction, we will recognize, is one of degree rather than of kind. Every effective plan employs some sanctions of the government and some sanctions of discrete individuals; that is, every plan requires of its human subjects some obedience and some rationality, the degree of each varying within limits that are set by the mediate norm. Hence in every society planning, to some degree, is both the obligation of the government and the right of discrete individuals. This proposition has been fundamental to the whole of this study.

[1]Henri Bergson, *Creative Evolution,* trans. by Arthur Mitchell (New York: Holt, Rinehart and Winston, Inc., 1911, 1939), p. 223.

Yet the assertion that every society has *a* plan may not seem wholly plausible. There should, of course, be no difficulty in interpreting, with respect to content, some of the empirical events in which human beings are involved as correlates of the plans of discrete individuals. All of us commonly speak of entrepreneurs' plans, consumers' plans, community plans, etc. In so doing we are in all truth *constructing* those plans ourselves; we are creating conceptual units, which we call *plans,* out of a universe of heterogeneous events. Why, then, should we not likewise speak of *plan* in the singular, interpreting some of the events in which human beings are involved, with respect to content, as correlates of *a* social plan? This procedure asks no more of our credulity than does that which we all employ when we impute plans to our own and to others' behavior. Both procedures involve the same epistemological assumptions. In both cases we impose a system of *a priori* categories upon a universe of events, thereupon discovering unity in those events.

Nineteenth-century America, for example, is commonly considered to have been an unplanned society. Yet, as the historian Hurst has shown, there was in that period a well-formulated system of economic priorities which governed the allocation of investment funds, whereby transportation, commercial agriculture, credit facilities, and industry—in that order—received legislative favor.[2] In this system, notes Hurst, ". . . government took the responsibility of channeling the flow of assets in some key areas of the economy and employed a variety of compulsions to this end."[3] Moreover, the dispersion of production and consumption which characterized the laissez-faire economy of that time was itself an expression of deliberate legislative policy; indeed, ". . . law guaranteed and protected individuals and groups

---

[2] James Willard Hurst, *Law and the Conditions of Freedom in the Nineteenth-Century United States* (Madison: University of Wisconsin Press, 1956; copyright by Northwestern University), pp. 53–54.

[3] *Ibid.,* p. 53.

in their private planning and execution, . . ."[4] In this conception of American economic development can be seen the empirical relevance of a system of *a priori* categories which make possible the interpretation of a particular universe of events as comprising elements of *a* plan.

The intent of this discussion has been to make these categories explicit. That purpose has been realized in the three devices of the basic legal norm (Kelsen), the basic economic norm, and the mediate norm. Kelsen's basic legal norm allows us to interpret a collection of legal statements as a valid normative order: the state. The basic economic norm allows us to interpret a collection of prices as another valid order: the market. The first of these orders constitutes the subject matter of jurisprudence; the second constitutes the subject matter of economics. The mediate norm makes its contribution by coordinating the prescribed and permitted events of the state and the market with the empirical events of the natural order, thus allowing us to specify the limits within which conjunctions of laws and prices can be valid. A plan is just such a conjunction. Thus it is the mediate norm which allows us to impose conceptual unity upon a collection of laws and prices, giving us a normative suborder which we call a *plan.*

The unity of a plan, then, whether it be the plan of a government or the plan of a single individual, is an artifact of three epistemological devices: the basic legal norm, the basic economic norm, and the mediate norm. These constructs are implicit in every reference that we make to planning, even though we are seldom if ever aware of them. The present study has only made explicit the basic categories which are presupposed in all knowledge of social and economic planning.

Basic to this analysis has been the Kantian distinction between the normative and the natural. It is only with this distinction, indeed, that we can sustain the idea of freedom in planning. The

---

[4] *Ibid.*

idea of freedom implies some degree of autonomy on the part of the human agent from the determinism of a natural order. Just such an autonomy is implied in planning. Within the limits of efficacy that are set by the mediate norm a plan is the free creation of the human agents who have been authorized by the two basic norms to create its norms. Those agents in turn, viewed as creatures of the two basic norms and the lower norms which derive therefrom, are perforce themselves free. Such freedom, of course, is conceivable only in terms of the epistemological categories by which a normative order is apprehended. It is conceivable only in terms of the discrepancy which obtains between the content of that order and the content of the natural order—a discrepancy large enough to manifest the autonomy of the one from the other, but not so large as to violate the conditions of efficacy set by the mediate norm. This relationship, we have seen, constitutes the phenomenon of conformity.

The systematic investigation of these phenomena defines the subject matter of planning, viewed now as an intellectual discipline. In this respect planning presents itself as both an art and a science. As art it is concerned with determining just which norms and activities will comply with the two basic norms. As science it is concerned with determining just which norms and activities will comply with the mediate norm. Both as art and as science, planning derives its subject matter from the conceptual categories which, once they have been made explicit, comprise the pure theory of planning.

INDEX

activities, anomalous: and extremity of sanctions, 78, 112, 113–114; invalidity of normative surrogates of, 112; relation of, to valid activities, 112–114; in nonstability plan, 112, 113, 114–115

activities, plan: propositions on relation of, to agent, 6; defined, 8; in hypothetical-conditional form of norms, 9; retrospective, 9; prospective, 9; law-price sanctions on, 59–60; and extremity of sanctions, 57–58, 65, 71–85, 95–97 *passim;* in effective plan, 75–85 *passim;* actual, 111; and anomolous activities, 78, 112–115

—, relation of, to behavioral activities. SEE plan, conformity to

— as economic: scarcity attribute of, 8–9; as concern of jurisprudence and economics, 14; relation of market and state control in, 28–29; basis for permitted, in market, 35; in capital, and efficacy, 99–100

—, efficacy of: relation of value to, 51, 53–55, 53 n., 56–58, 57 n., 62–63, 68–69, 69, 75–85 *passim;* mediate norm in determining, 56, 58, 67, 75, 85, 119; as condition for validity, 75, 79, 81–82; and extremity of sactions, 80–85 *passim,* 95–98 *passim*

—, nonobservance of. SEE sanctions

—, types of. SEE allocative plans; compensatory plans; developmental plans; stability plans; structural plans

—, valid: defined, 4; lattice theory in identifying, 70–85 *passim;* types of, 82–86; behavioral versions of, 99, 104, 105 (table); obedience and rationality required for, 98 and n.; in actual plans, 111; demands of, and anomalous activities, 112–114

—, validity of: conditions for, in *Planwirtschaft,* 22; basic legal and economic norms in determining, 51, 53, 68; value as condition of, 55–56, 58–59, 64, 68, 85; of contract and government plan in state and market, 68; efficacy as condition of, 75, 79, 81–83. SEE ALSO norm, basic economic; norm, basic legal

—, value of: defined, 50–51; mediate norm in determining, 51–55, 56–59, 57 n., 65, 75; relation of, to efficacy, 51, 53–55, 53 n., 56–58, 57 n., 64, 69, 75–85 *passim;* and normative-natural relation, 51–55, 56–58, 65, 75–84 *passim;* agents ascribing, 56; as condition for validity, 55–56, 58–59, 64, 68, 85; in determining state-market overlap, 60–65, 68, 69–70; as asymmetrical, 64–65, 84; in identifying valid plan, 65, 66, 68–85 *passim;* of contract and governmental plan, in state and market, 68, 85; lattice theory applied to, 70–85 *passim;* in stability planning, 71, 84; in individ-

mative order, relation of, to natural order

Eléments d'économie politique pure: 31–32

Epicureans, the: 13

equilibrium, economic: in economic thought, 32–33; Walras' theory of, 34–36, 34 n., 37–42, 39 n.; limitations of Walras' theory of, 42–43; and governmental plans, 44; mentioned, 101, 105, 108

events, plan: 8. SEE ALSO activities, plan

fa chia (legalist school): 13

free-will: in planning, 3, 4–5, 10–11, 48–50, 65, 87–88, 118–119

Frege, Fredrich Ludwig Gottlob: 10

Glaucon: 12

government. SEE planner, government as; plans, governmental

Greeks, the: 3

harmony, natural: 32–33

Hicks, John R.: 33, 38

history, economic: 14

Hobbes, Thomas: 12, 19

Hurst, James Willard: on planning in nineteenth-century America, 117

incentives: normative character of, 5–6, 7; as permissive propositions, 6–7; sanctions in, 7–8; economic nature of, 15

India: 13

individualism: 13

interest, rate of: in stability plans, 101, 103; in individual developmental plans, 104, 105; in governmental developmental plans, 107; in individual allocative plans, 109; in governmental allocative plans, 110

investment: process of, as capital formation, 99–100; lending and borrowing in, 100; relation of, to sanctions, 100; consequences of, 100; in stability plans, 100–103

passim; in individual developmental plans, 104–107 *passic*; in governmental developmental plans, 107–109; in individual allocative plans, 109–110; in governmental allocative plans, 110–111

invisible-hand theory: 32–33

Isnard, Achille-Nicolas: 33

Jellinek, Georg: *normative Kraft des Faktischen*, 55–56

jurisprudence: 13, 118

—, analytical: conception of normative order of, 13–15; obligation in, 14; individual and collectivity in, 14–15; planning as branch of, 15, 16. SEE ALSO law

Kant, Immanuel: 8, 10

Kautilya: 13

Kelsen, Hans. SEE law, Kelsen's pure theory of

Keynes, John Maynard: 33

laissez faire: 13

lattice theory: in identifying valid plan activities, 70–85 *passim*

law: as normative order, 19; correspondence of, with actual events, 19; as command of sovereign, 20; the state as, 21. SEE ALSO jurisprudence

—, Kelsen's pure theory of: on efficacy in normative order, 4 and n.; on validity in normative order, 4–5, 4 n.; relation of normative and natural order in, 5, 20–21; sanctions in, 7, 8, 20, 21; hypothetical-conditional character of legal norms in, 7, 20; enforcement by collectivity (government) in, 13, 19, 20–21 and n., 45; in analyzing plan as legal order, 16, 18; unity of legal norms in, 21; the state in, 21; and *Planwirtschaft* economy, 21–22; transaction in, 26–28, 45; legal order as self-limiting in, 28–29, 45; mentioned, 10, 31, 33, 36, 37, 47, 51. SEE ALSO norm, basic legal; norms, legal; state (legal order)

laws. SEE norms, legal; sanctions; state-market overlap

legal order. SEE state (legal order)

legal transaction. SEE contract (legal transaction)

liberalism: 13

Locke, John: utilitarianism-natural harmony blending by, 32

market (economic order): and validity of incentives, 15; as normative order, 15–16, 28–29, 32, 34 n., 34–36, 41; individual as planner of, 16, 32–39 *passim*, 41–46 *passim*; equilibrium in, 33, 34–35, 36, 38 n., 38–40, 42–44; amalgamation in, 34–35, 36, 38, 40–41; norms of, 35–36; efficacy of, 32, 40; as set of valid prices, 36, 39–40; planning theory implied in, 36, 40–41; validity of norms of, 36, 38–40; efficacy of, and validity of norms, 37; unity of, and basic economic norm, 37–38, 40; unity of, and valid norms, 40; limitations of, 42–45, 59; in stability plans, 100. SEE ALSO economics; economy; norm, basic economic; prices; state-market overlap

Marx, Karl: 13

mediate norm. SEE norm, mediate

Mercantilists, the: 12

natural law: 13, 19

natural order. SEE normative order, relation of, to natural order

nonstability plans: nonconformity in, 115. SEE ALSO allocative plans; developmental plans

norm. SEE norm, basic economic; norm, basic legal; norm, mediate; norms, economic; norms, legal; norms, plan

norm, basic economic: statement of, 37; and validity of economic norms (prices), 37–39, 40–41, 45, 53, 118; and unity of economic norms (market), 37–39, 118; power of agent in, 45, 46; in efficacy of

normative order, 40, 45–46; natural-normative relation in, 40, 53, 88; sanctions in, 41–42; in validity of contracts, 42–44, 67–68; in validity of governmental plans, 44, 67–68; sanctions of, and behavior, 88–89 and n., 95, 96; in completely effective normative order, 88–90, 89 and n. SEE ALSO norm, basic legal, and basic economic norm; planner, individual as; prices; rationality

norm, basic legal: in unity of plan norms (legal order), 22–23, 24–25, 29, 118; in validity of plan norms (laws), 22–26 *passim*, 27, 28, 29, 38, 51, 53, 118; basis for validity of, 25, 88; statement of, 25 and n.; and normative-natural relation, 25–26, 29–30, 52, 53, 88; agent of authority in, 25–26, 28, 44, 46; and efficacy of normative order (plan), 25–26, 29–30, 45, 46, 88; in validity of contracts, 29, 42, 44, 67–68; in validity of governmental plan, 44–45, 67–68; in completely effective normative order, 88–89; sanctions of, and behavior, 88–89, 95–96. SEE ALSO norms, legal; obedience; planner, government as

— and basic economic norm: inconsistency between lesser norms of, 59; in validity of contract and governmental plan, 44, 67–68; correspondence of normative with natural order in, 88; and normative surrogates of anomalous activities, 112; in constructing categories for planning, 118; and planning as an art, 119

norm, mediate: statement of, 54–55; in determining obedience and rationality limits, 56, 59, 85; in coordinating empirical and plan events, 56, 58, 65–85, 118; and planning as art and science, 56, 118; refinement of statement of, 56–59; and freedom in planning, 65; in establishing plan as normative suborder, 67, 118; in revealing unity

in plan, 67, 85, 118; in defining
dual affiliation of contracts and governmental plans, 67–68; behavioral
rendition of, 75–76, 95; and agent
of effective planning, 86
— in determining value of activity:
and natural and normative concerns
of basic norm, 51–55; and correspondence of value and efficacy, 53–
55, 53 n., 58–59, 65, 69, 75, 78,
81–82; and determining activities
of effective plan, 56, 58, 69, 71, 75–
85; and relation of value and validity, 55–56, 58–59, 81–82, 85;
clauses in, arranged according to
efficacy, 56–58, 57 n.; on agent of
value ascription, 56; clauses in, arranged according to sanction extremity, 57–58; and determining
valid norms, 58–59, 71–85; to
identify respective state-market portions in valid plan, 59–60, 67–85,
118; and minimal and maximal
values for valid plan, 60–63, 64,
65; and possible types of state-
market intersections, 63–64; and
activities of asymmetrical value,
64–65, 84, 118; and necessary
values for effective plan, 66–85;
lattice theory applied to, 70–85
passim; in types of planning, 71–
75; and relation of sanctions to
efficacy, 76–84 *passim, 95*
normative order: law (the state) as,
19–22, 28–29, 44–45, 118; affiliation of contract in dual, 26–27, 42–
44, 67–68; relation of state and
market as, 28–29, 46, 59–60, 65,
118; market as, 32, 33–36, 40–41,
44–45, 118; affiliation of governmental plan in dual, 44, 67–68; as
domain of art, 49; validity of events
in, 49. SEE ALSO plan; state-market
overlap
—, effective: concern of jurisprudence
and economics with, 13–14; value
as indicator of conditions for, 58–
59; mediate norm in determining,
67; types of activities in, 69, 75,

79, 81–85, 86; relations of sanction and behavior in, 76–79, 80–
84, 89–90, 92–94; and validity, 87;
basic norms in, 88–89, 88 n. SEE
ALSO activities, plan, efficacy of;
normative order, relation of, to
natural order; plan, conformity to;
planner
—, plan as: by definition, 4, 15, 17,
22; and nature of propositions, 5–8,
12; and value of plan activities, 22;
and validity of norms, 22–26 *passim*; and plan unity, 22; dual normative status of, 44, 47, 60; within
state-market overlap, 46–47; obedience and rationality in effective, 47.
SEE ALSO normative order, relation
of, to natural order; plan, conformity to; state-market overlap
—, relation of, to natural order: and
free-will determinism problem, 3–5,
10–11, 26, 48–50, 87, 118–119; and
validity of plan, 4, 49, 87–88; and
efficacy of plan, 4, 5, 87–88; as
correspondence in plan, 5, 50, 87–
88; in plan events, 8; in retrospective activities, 9; in plan norms, 10;
in relation of norms and behavior,
17; in theories of law, 19–21; and
validity of norms, 22, 23, 25–26,
37, 40, 79, 87–88; and power of
agents, 27–28, 45; basic norms in
coordinating, 29–30, 32, 40, 45, 46,
51–52, 53 and n., 59, 88; in the
state, 29; and range of "can" and
"ought to be," 30; and combination
of obedience and rationality, 47, 87;
in effective plan, 47, 48–50; in effective order, 49–50; value in cor-
relating, 50–51, 53–54, 55, 56–59,
57 n., 65, 75, 83, 84, 85; and
mediate norm, 53–55, 56–59, 57 n.,
65, 67, 85, 118, 119; as limiting
state-market overlap for effective
plans, 68–69; and activities real-
izable in natural order, 75, 79,
81–83; and relation of sanctions
and behavior, 76–79, 80–84, 88–
115 *passim*. SEE ALSO normative